A VISUAL HISTORY OF
SCIENCE AND
TECHNOLOGY

ROSEN PUBLISHING

ALBERTO HERNÁNDEZ

This edition published in 2017 by
The Rosen Publishing Group, Inc.
29 East 21st Street
New York, NY 10010

Library of Congress Cataloging-in-Publication Data

Names: Hernández, Alberto, author.
Title: A visual history of science and technology / Alberto Hernández.
Description: New York : Rosen Publishing, 2017. | Series: A visual history of the world | Audience: Grades 7 to 12. | Includes bibliographical references and index.
Identifiers: LCCN 2016035116 | ISBN 9781499465969 (library bound)
Subjects: LCSH: Science—History—Juvenile literature. | Technology—History—Juvenile literature.
Classification: LCC Q126.4 .F38 2017 | DDC 509—dc23
LC record available at https://lccn.loc.gov/2016035116

Manufactured in Malaysia

Metric Conversion Chart

1 inch = 2.54 centimeters; 25.4 millimeters	1 cup = 250 milliliters
1 foot = 30.48 centimeters	1 ounce = 28 grams
1 yard = .914 meters	1 fluid ounce = 30 milliliters
1 square foot = .093 square meters	1 teaspoon = 5 milliliters
1 square mile = 2.59 square kilometers	1 tablespoon = 15 milliliters
1 ton = .907 metric tons	1 quart = .946 liters
1 pound = 454 grams	355 degrees F = 180 degrees Celsius
1 mile = 1.609 kilometers	

©2016 Editorial Sol90
Barcelona – Buenos Aires
All Rights Reserved
Editorial Sol90, S.L

Original Idea Nuria Cicero
Editorial Coordination Alberto Hernández
Editorial Team Alberto Moreno de la Fuente, Luciana Rosende, Virginia Iris Fernández, Pablo Pineau, Matías Loewy, Joan Soriano, Mar Valls, Leandro Jema
Proofreaders Marta Kordon, Edgardo D'Elio
Design María Eugenia Hiriart
Layout Laura Ocampo, Clara Miralles, Paola Fornasaro

Photography Age Fotostock, Getty Images, Science Photo Library, National Geographic, Latinstock, Album, ACI, Cordon Press
Illustrations and Infographics Trexel Animation, Trebol Animation,

WOW Studio, Sebastián Giacobino, Néstor Taylor, Nuts Studio, Steady in Lab, 3DN, Federico Combi, Pablo Aschei, Leonardo César, 4D News, Rise Studio, Ariel Roldán, Dorian Vandegrift, Zoom Desarrollo Digitales, Marcelo Regalado.

Contents

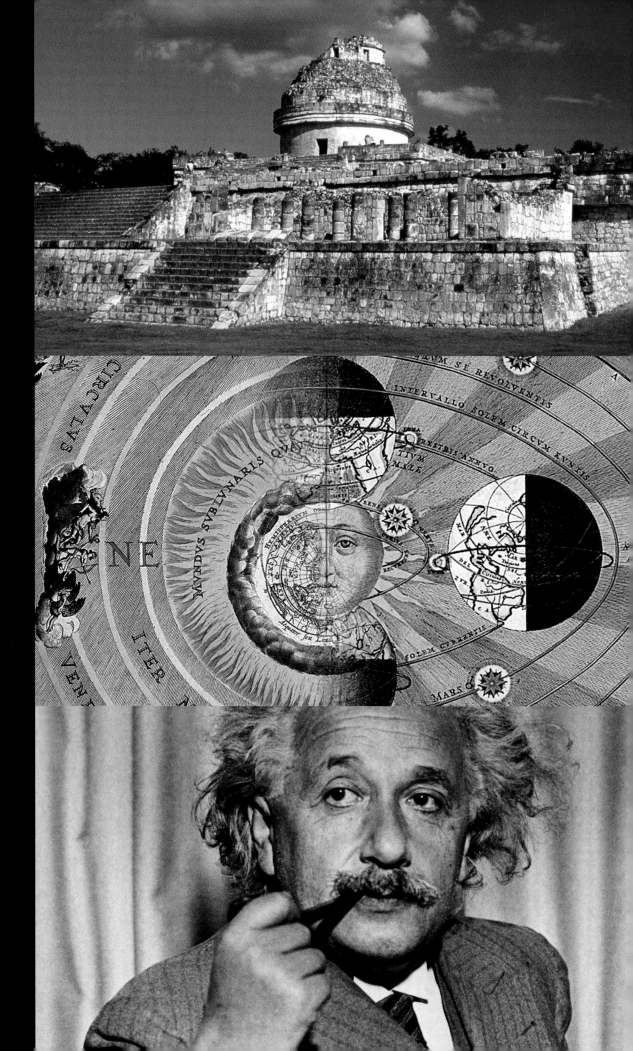

Introduction

The great ancient Greek philosophers, Pythagoras, Democritus , Aristotle and Euclid to name a few, were the ones who started the road of scientific development in the Western World. In some cases, their **contributions** could be demonstrated after many centuries (e.g. the atomism of Democritus, Aristarchus' heliocentrism) or were in effect for two millennia, such as Euclidean geometry. It was not until the Renaissance and the Modern Age that a science advancement of such magnitude took place again with the **Copernican revolution** of the sixteenth century. Going from the static geocentric model of the solar system to a heliocentric solar system is considered the **starting point** of the Scientific Revolution, which finally started in the seventeenth century, with Galileo Galilei, Johannes Kepler and later **Isaac Newton**, the father of modern science and classical physics.

In the eighteenth century, chemistry began its path, and in the nineteenth century **Charles Darwin** revolutionized biology by discovering that the human being had apelike ancestors. The Darwinian theory of natural selection was soon supplemented by Gregor Mendel's laws of inheritance, a discipline that gained increasing prominence. In the last century, **Albert Einstein**, by means of his theories of **special relativity** (1905) and general relativity (1915), exceeded the Newtonian physics with his astonishing discoveries about the curvature of spacetime, the mass-energy equivalence and the photoelectric effect, among many others.

By the second half of the twentieth century, after pursuing and achieving the development of the atomic bomb, man walked on the **Moon** and technique led to technologies. Technoscience emerged from the fusion of said technologies with science, which has established solid ground for computers, Internet and critical projects as the decoding of the **human genome**. Biomedicine has also given giant steps. However, this extraordinary development in few decades has fueled a rapid growth that creates new problems while addressing others from the past, feeding the debate on **ethics** as regards science and the development of scientific activism and environmentalism.

Chronology

830
▶ AL-KHWARIZMI
The Persian mathematician, astronomer and geographer Al-Khwarizmi developed algebra and spread the Arabic number system.

1530
▶ HELIOCENTRISM
The astronomer Nicolaus Copernicus proposed the heliocentric model, deepening the theory conceived by Aristarchus of Samos in 250 BC.

V–IV BC
▶ MODERN SCIENCE
The treaties of the Greek Hippocrates of Cos are the starting point of modern medicine and science itself in the strict sense.

VI BC
▶ PYTHAGORAS
The Pythagoreans developed the Pythagorean Theorem in Greece.

V BC
▶ ATOMISM
Leucippus and his pupil Democritus formulated the atomic theory in Greece: everything is made of atoms, indivisible particles separated by a vacuum.

300 BC
▶ EUCLID
Euclid, the Greek mathematician, wrote his famous work *Elements* setting the foundations of classical geometry, which were in force until the 19th century.

1687

▶ GRAVITY

Isaac Newton published *Principia Mathematica*, which sets out the law of universal gravitation and lays the foundations of classical mechanics in the so-called Newton's laws.

1928

▶ ANTIBIOTICS

The Scot Alexander Fleming discovered penicillin, the first antibiotic of general use in medicine.

1969

▶ TRIP TO THE MOON

The U.S. mission Apollo 11 reaches the Moon and man walks on said satellite for the first time.

1600

▶ GALILEO GALILEI

With his theory of the inclined plane, Galileo Galilei buried the cornerstones of Aristotelian physics.

1619

▶ KEPLER'S LAWS

Johannes Kepler completed his Laws of planetary motion with the publication of the last law in his work *Harmonices Mundi*.

1859

▶ EVOLUTION

Charles Darwin set out his theory of evolution for the human species through natural selection in *The Origin of Species*.

1915

▶ RELATIVITY

Albert Einstein published the general theory of relativity, which replaced Newton's theory of gravity. It was the greatest advance in science since the advent of Newtonian laws.

1991

▶ WWW

The World Wide Web (WWW) was born, which definitely popularized Internet. One year later, there already existed a million computers.

2003

▶ THE HUMAN GENOME MAP

The human genome sequencing project was concluded, being the most significant biomedical research project in history.

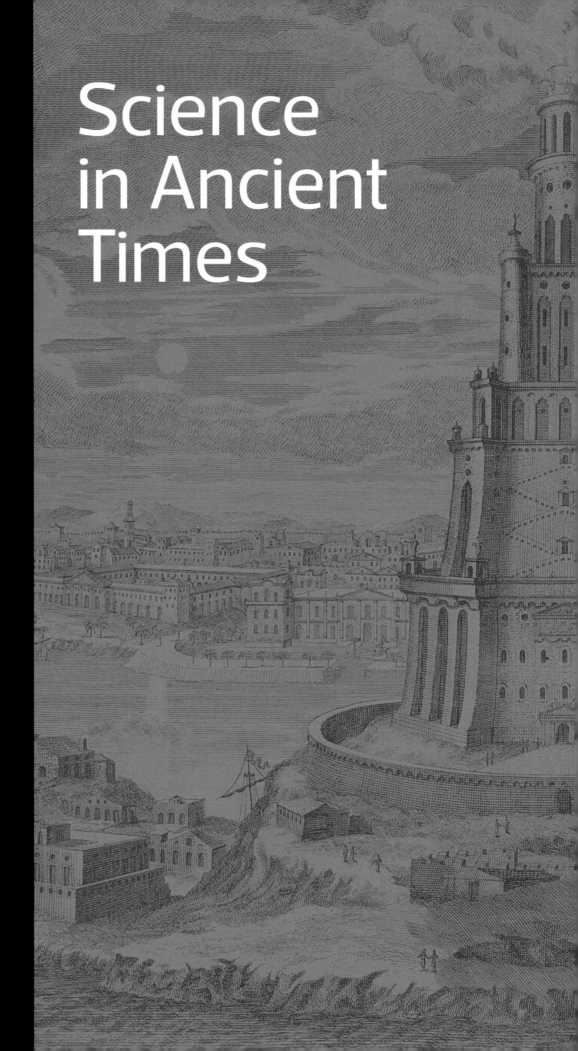

Chapter 1

Science in Ancient Times

When does the history of science really begin? For some historians, the manufacture of tools by *Homo sapiens* was already a scientific activity and so was the knowledge of nature acquired by Neolithic cultures. However, it was not until the arrival of the great civilizations that knowledge approaches experimentation. The change occurs in Ancient Greece when science emancipates from philosophy with the emergence of the empirical foundation in the Greek medical school, the most relevant figure of which is Hippocrates.

This does not detract from the knowledge of mathematics, astronomy and medicine that was acquired earlier in Greece itself, or in Mesopotamia, Egypt and China. The probable date of introduction of the Egyptian calendar, linked to the comprehension of floods and falls of the Nile, is very early: 4236 BC. On the other hand, in Mesopotamia, a decimal system was used supplemented with another sexagesimal system for numbers greater than 59 in 3000 BC, and positioning was used in writing numbers. In China, the detailed star map created by Zhang Heng in the second century AD collected about 2,500 stars, many more than those recorded by the Greek Hipparchus in his catalog of two centuries before, unknown to the Chinese scientist.

What Is Science?

A set of verified and structured knowledge is grouped under this term that allow deducing general laws or principles, which have been obtained by humans through observation and reasoning.

The Need to Know

Historically, humans have asked questions and sought answers. Science is responsible for obtaining and organizing this knowledge, once its veracity is proven through experimentation. In other words, science attempts to explain why certain events occur, how they occur or why they occur that way and not another. It locates the unique facts in general guidelines, and vice versa.

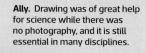

Ally. Drawing was of great help for science while there was no photography, and it is still essential in many disciplines.

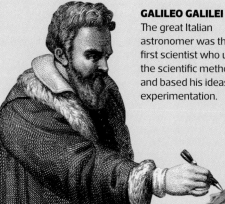

GALILEO GALILEI
The great Italian astronomer was the first scientist who used the scientific method and based his ideas in experimentation.

From Myth to Scientific Revolution

In the 16th and 17th centuries, science left behind ancient myths and medieval alchemy and started its modern phase with the Scientific Revolution, embodied in the figures of Nicholas Copernicus, Galileo Galilei and at a later time Isaac Newton. The application of the scientific method, which transformed science, began at this time.

The Scientific Method

This is the research procedure that follows science to produce knowledge and it is based on two fundamental principles: the reproducibility, –anyone can repeat an experiment anywhere– and refutability – you can check its false nature–. The scientific method can be summarized in four points:

1 Observation
Sensory study and description in detail of a phenomenon that arouses our curiosity.

2 Hypothesis
Development of one or more hypotheses to explain this phenomenon, i.e. its causality.

3 Demonstration
Checking hypotheses experimentally in order to ratify or discard them.

4 Conclusions
Extraction of a theory from tested hypotheses, or of a law, if they are repeated regularly.

TECHNOLOGY
Science and technology have mutually provided feedback throughout history. The development of one allowed the advance of the other and vice versa.

From Thales to Technoscience

The scientific knowledge gained by the oldest major civilizations of history, Mesopotamia and Egypt, were followed by the early Greek philosophers and Chinese technical advances. Thales of Miletus (624–546 BC) opened the path of the scientific journey that leads to the most recent discoveries, such as the human genome map.

Branches of Science

Usually, the sciences are divided into: natural (studying nature), social or human (dealing with human beings and their relationships), and formal. The first two are factual, i.e. they study empirical phenomena. The formal sciences, however, use the deduction as a method of seeking truth. This is the case of mathematics.

Sciences and Borders

Should we consider medicine as a natural or social science? It depends on its speciality. Anatomy would be a natural science, but bioethics could be considered social.

Anatomy. Engraving of Andreas Vesalius, the founder of modern anatomy.

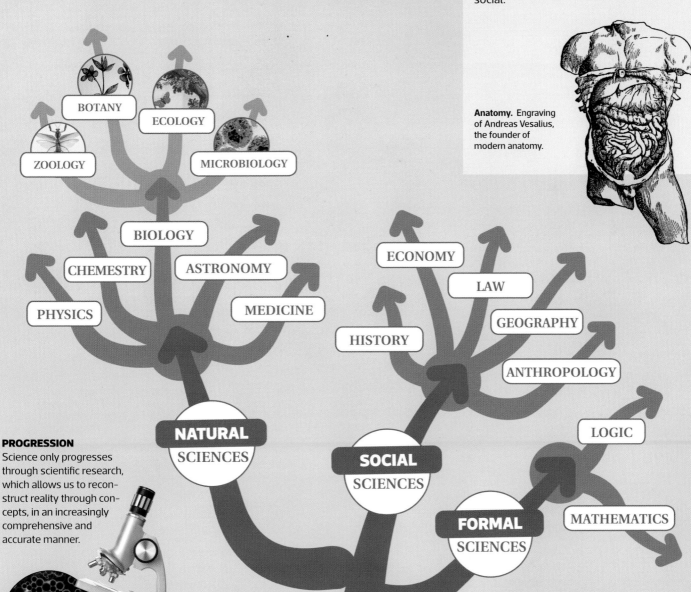

PROGRESSION
Science only progresses through scientific research, which allows us to reconstruct reality through concepts, in an increasingly comprehensive and accurate manner.

BOTANY

ECOLOGY

ZOOLOGY

MICROBIOLOGY

BIOLOGY

CHEMESTRY

ASTRONOMY

PHYSICS

MEDICINE

ECONOMY

LAW

HISTORY

GEOGRAPHY

ANTHROPOLOGY

LOGIC

MATHEMATICS

NATURAL SCIENCES

SOCIAL SCIENCES

FORMAL SCIENCES

Classification. As the number of disciplines is too high, the chart only shows some exemplary science of each branch.

Knowledge in Prehistory

In order to ensure their livelihood, prehistoric humans had to transmit to their offspring a set of crucial knowledge, as the control of fire and the use of tools for hunting. That is how teaching was born.

Learning and Observation

Historically, each generation has tried to pass on their knowledge and skills to the next. During prehistory, the lessons were brief and the knowledge and skills were learned through practice: there were no differences between "doing" and "learning." The adults explained to the children what they knew through movements and children imitated them until they achieved a successful execution. As early as the Neolithic, the progressive division of labor generated more and more knowledge.

Daily Activities. This illustration reconstructs learning moments in everyday life during prehistoric times.

FISHING
An adult accompanying a child that tries to fish in a river. The child helps to hold the rope attached to the spear.

Rites

One of the first educational practices found in every culture in the world is the initiation rite, ceremonies usually involving the passage from childhood to adulthood. They included teaching of essential knowledge for the community in question.

Stonehenge. Recreation of a rite within the Neolithic site.

Oral Communication

The transmission of knowledge in prehistoric times was done on a purely oral manner. Some traditional knowledge was communicated through legends, folklore, rituals and songs, without the need for a writing system.

Hordes

During prehistory, individuals were constantly on the move for food, grouped into hordes of about 20 to about 40 members to better ensure survival. Some tasks were divided by gender: males were responsible for hunting and fishing, and females, for picking fruits and vegetables.

HUNTERS
Although it was customary to feed on small mammals, men hunted large animals such as bison, bears or mammoths.

Tools

The development and use of tools for hunting and fishing was essential knowledge in prehistory. They manufactured weapons, spears, needles, traps...

COLLECTION
The properties and hazards of the fruits and vegetables were among the first concepts that were transmitted.

MANUFACTURING
A child tries to polish two stones copying what he learned from an adult, who guides him in his attempt.

STONE WORK
The stone was polished by rubbing it with another stone or object.

Science in Mesopotamia

The Mesopotamians, who formed the first great civilization in history, were pioneers in astrology and astronomy. Their astronomical observations led them to develop a calendar and to flourish very remarkably in math.

Development of Knowledge

Between 3100 and 332 BC, Sumerians, Akkadians, Babylonians and other Mesopotamian peoples reached an outstanding scientific level. Their handling of numbers and the abundance of mathematical calculations found in the clay tablets that have survived until today, which contain examples of a profuse record of data and operations related with daily activities, is surprising. Their systematisation of weights and measures was a major step toward modern science.

Geometry. Calculation of the surface of a parcel of land. It dates back to 2100 BC.

Mathematical Achievements

The Mesopotamians used the decimal system until number 59 completed with another sexagesimal from 60 onwards. They were familiar with the positional notation, unknown to the Greeks and Romans, since the third millennium BC, and they employed multiplication and division. In geometry, they measured fields and buildings accurately, and divided the circle into 360 degrees.

CONSTELLATIONS
They cataloged 37 constellations and established the 12 signs of the zodiac.

The Medicine

The diseases and illnesses in Mesopotamia were considered divine punishment. For healing they, they resorted to magicians, the *ashipu*, or to the *asu*, who used medicinal herbs. In these practices, concepts such as medical revision, diagnosis and the prescription of recipes were applied.

Pazuzu. The Mesopotamians believed that the demon Pazuzu -here, in a 1000 BC figure- was the carrier of diseases.

SCRIBES
The scribe-priests or *sanga* wrote the religious, literary and scientific knowledge on clay tablets.

With Both Hands

The sexagesimal calculation stems from the way of counting with both hands: with one hand they reached up to 12 using the three phalanges of each finger (except the thumb). Upon reaching number 12, they extended a finger of the other hand to remember those 12 units and they began again.

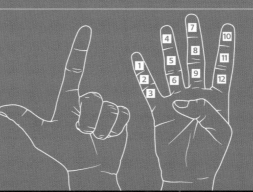

Example. The left hand indicates we reached 12 twice (hence, 24). The thumb of the other hand serves to identify numbers of 1 to 12 , which would be added to 24.

Great Astronomers

The Mesopotamians developed a calendar from which we still use some elements, such as the division of the year into 12 months and the day into 24 hours. We also owe them division of the hour into 60 minutes and of the minute into 60 seconds. They knew the ecliptic, and determined the cycles of appearance of solar and lunar eclipses.

REMARKS
They examined the movement of the Sun, the planetary conjunctions and the positions of stars, among others.

Tools

In Mesopotamia, they invented the sundial (sun clock in a plane), the clepsydra (water clock) and the *polos*, a perfected quadrant that allowed reading the time at night from the position of the stars.

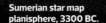

Sumerian star map planisphere, 3300 BC.

THE PRIEST *BARU*
He was a soothsayer or religious operator who interpreted signs from heaven as omens. He had knowledge of mathematics, astronomy and religion.

Science in Egypt

Over three thousand years ago, ancient Egyptians acquired important scientific knowledge. They were noteworthy in medicine and mathematics, and engineering of course, but also staged major advances in astronomy and chemistry.

Water and Sun

Towards the fifth millennium BC, Egyptians had developed irrigated agriculture and by the third millennium BC, they had built a vast network of canals and dams. From the periodicity of the flooding of the Nile and stargazing, before the fourth millennium BC, a calendar of 365 days was created with a leap year, which was used to calculate the trail of the sun and to divide the year into three seasons of four months: from June to September, flooding, from October to February, planting, and from February to June, collection.

FRACTURES

In the construction works, fractures were common and to treat them flints and bandages were applied. Techniques were also developed to suture wounds and stop bleeding.

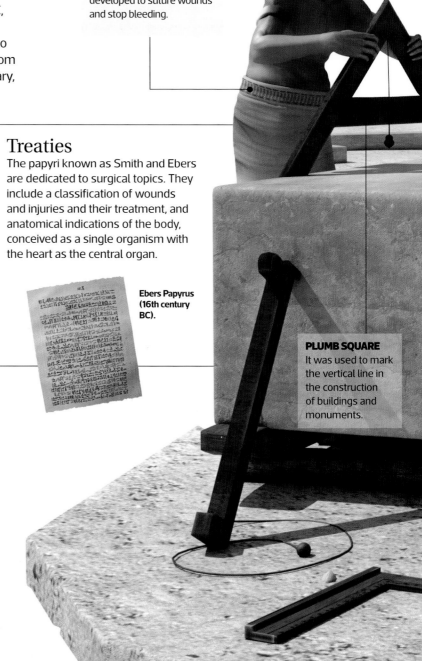

Surgical Instruments

Surgery was practiced by doctors using flint, metal or finely crafted and polished bone tools. Circumcision was practiced regularly, it is believed that wound were sutured and some murals illustrate on skull trepanation techniques.

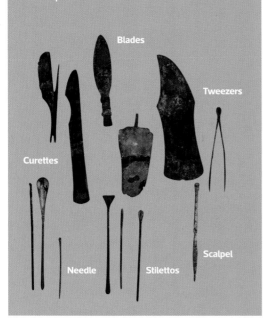

Blades

Tweezers

Curettes

Needle

Stilettos

Scalpel

Treaties

The papyri known as Smith and Ebers are dedicated to surgical topics. They include a classification of wounds and injuries and their treatment, and anatomical indications of the body, conceived as a single organism with the heart as the central organ.

Ebers Papyrus (16th century BC).

PLUMB SQUARE

It was used to mark the vertical line in the construction of buildings and monuments.

Physicians

The Egyptian state financed doctors or *Sum-Un*, "men of the suffering." The rules of learning and practicing medicine were established by the physician of the Pharaoh. He was followed in hierarchy by the physicians of the court, the medical examiners and practicing physicians. In addition, there were doctors who specialized in assisting workers, doctors of the church and the army, etc.

HESY-RA
Specialist in dental diseases, Hesy-Ra (2649-2575 BC), in the picture, was head of the medical school of the Egyptian court.

Calculations

In order to erect the pyramids, divide land or calculate the distance to the Sun, the Egyptians used mathematics with great practicality. The so-called Rhind papyrus (17th century BC) contains 87 problems and their solutions, with exercises of arithmetic, geometry and measurement (calculation of areas, concepts of trigonometry, etc.).

PAPYRUS
This writing surface – used up to the second century, when it was replaced by parchments– allowed the Egyptians to record scientific knowledge.

NUMBERING
They used a decimal system of notation with signs for 1, 10, 100, 1,000, 10,000 and 100,000. A small vertical line represented a unit.

Transmitting Knowledge

The history of humankind begins with the written record of knowledge and of the details of the life of peoples. Writing, which emerged in Mesopotamia more than 5,000 years ago, facilitated the transfer of knowledge to future generations.

Towards Simplification

The creation of the first alphabet took place nearly a millennium after writing and it is believed that Semitic peoples settled in the Egyptian Sinai -Jews, Assyrians, Carthaginians among many others- were the ones who developed it. The appearance of the alphabet represented the simplification of writing, a field which for centuries was only accessed by a select few, like the Egyptian scribes.

Alphabet Progress

After the appearance of the Proto-Semitic alphabet towards 2000 BC, the Phoenicians, trading people par excellence of the Mediterranean, would be the ones who developed their own alphabet a millennium later.
By 800 BC, it was the turn of the Greek alphabet, which use spread throughout the same region and was adapted by the Etruscans, originating the Latin alphabet we know today.

Ancient Egypt 3000 BC	Proto-Semitic 2000 BC	Phoenician 1100 BC
Symbol	Symbol	Symbol

Greek alphabet 800-600 BC

Early · Classical Modern

Etruscan alphabet 700 BC

Symbol · Early

Modern

PROPER STANCE
The scribes would sit cross-legged. They placed a table over them and the papyrus in which they wrote on top of it. Some worked squat.

QUILL TO WRITE
It was a hollow reed obliquely cut which was dipped in vegetal inks.

Information Registration

Information management has been vital to the human intellectual growth. Throughout history, the techniques for writing, collection and storage of information have changed, but not the importance of having reliable data.

ROMANS NOTARIES
The involvement of these officials gave public character to private documents. Their signature or affixing their seal was enough.

FROM THE NILE TO THE SCRIBES
The papyrus was obtained from a namesake plant growing on the Nile.

Respected by All

The scribes were revered writing specialists that documented every social event and also classified, counted and copied all kinds of information. They belonged to the state administration and their profession was essential for kings and government officials. As most people were illiterate, the capabilities of the scribes were admired and well remunerated economically. In Egypt, three types of writing were used: hieroglyphic, demotic and hieratic.

OFFICIALS
In the case of Egypt, the scribes belonged to the state administration. Their work was essential.

DEPOSITARIES
The scribes were in charge of guarding the intellectual production of Egypt.

WRITING
It evolved through the centuries. In Egypt, the oldest type was the hieroglyphic writing, with a sacred nature.

INKS
Red or black inks were distributed on a palette. They were made with natural extracts.

Writing Surfaces

Around 40,000 years ago, Paleolithic men began to convey messages on stone by pigments or carvings. Thus began a vertiginous progress that has reached developments that were unimaginable for said humans.

Connections

We can establish connections with prehistoric men through pictorial messages that have been immortalized on the walls of caves. We know about the ancient civilizations of Mesopotamia, China and Egypt, thanks to their legacy present in clay and wood tablets, and papyrus. The aspirations and fears of the Middle Ages reach us through the parchment and, as from the invention of the printing press in the fifteenth century, we count with the cultural heritage of Humanity on paper. With the computer age, filed data has increased to levels difficult to conceive.

The Evolution of Media

Over the centuries, writing media went from being fixed and heavy, to lighter each time, until paper was invented. In recent years, the advent of electronic devices has improved storage capacity, among other advantages.

Colleting Knowledge

The use of papyrus provided, among other things, the creation, conveyance and storage of manuscripts. In Alexandria, a library was built which became the largest library of Ancient Times, the walls of which housed more than 900,000 volumes. Symbol of Hellenic thought, wise men and students visited it from far away, such as Archimedes, Euclid and Galen.

The modern library of Alexandria. Launched in 2002, its construction has been promoted by UNESCO.

40 000 BC	3200 BC	3000 BC	1500 BC
Stone	**Clay**	**Papyrus**	**Parchment**
Stone was the first registered writing surface where man made his mark since Paleolithic times, using different types of pigments.	The earliest recorded means of writing were made with wedge-shaped objects on wet clay tablets in Mesopotamia.	One of the great inventions of Ancient Egypt, then became universal. It was produced from vegetable fiber extracted from the namesake plant.	Generated from animal leather by a special treatment. It replaced the papyrus since it allowed to making corrections.

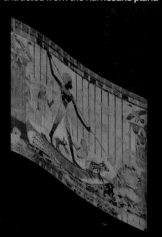

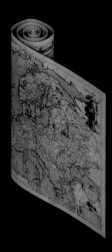

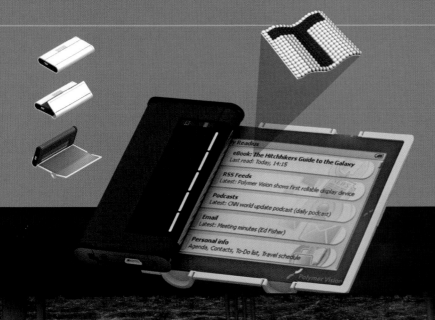

Electronic Ink

It is the technology used by modern electronic books or e-books. Based on microcapsules that can be stimulated electronically, it allows having screens thinner than a credit card, which can be folded .

THE BOOK
After Gutenberg introduced movable type printing in Europe towards 1450, the book became the great universal means for writing.

Rivalries

Legend has it that Ptolemy VI –picture–, king of Hellenistic Egypt, felt enormous jealousy for the library of Pergamum and banned the export of papyrus to that Greek polis. The king of Pergamon, Eunemes II, devised parchment to replace it. The use of this new media spread around the Mediterranean.

Second century

Paper
It emerged in China in the second century. It did not reach Europe until eight centuries later. Its use was multiplied with the advent of the printing press in Europe.

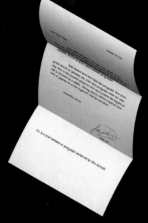

Twentieth century

Tablets and e-books
In the late twentieth century, various electronic devices were developed to allow storing and displaying large amounts of text and images.

The Origins of Medicine

In the sedentary tribes of prehistory, a member of the group would specialize in healing tasks, which were often covered by divine influences. Over time, medicine moved away from religious practices.

The Force of Reason

The practice of medicine in Mesopotamia and Egypt, two of the ancient civilizations which documented it, was related to religious beliefs and spirits. This also happened in the early civilizations of the Indus, where demonic exorcisms were common. In ancient China, Taoist physicians were the first to develop an observation that explained diseases as an expression of the natural order of the universe. The Greeks were mainly the ones who would apply reason in the search for treatments in science, and not religion.

PROFESSIONALS
The physicians performed clinical practices using remedies, instruments and prayers to the gods.

Egyptian Physicians

Remunerated by the State, Egyptian doctors were highly respected people who occupied their days between medical research and direct care. Apart from being the first surgeons in history, it is believed that they cured certain types of cancer and also performed cranial trepanation.

INSTRUMENTS
The precise surgical tools were perfected thanks to the knowledge of mummification.

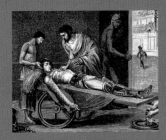

Claudius Galen, pioneer

This second-century Greek physician, one of the fathers of medicine, was the first to perform eye and brain surgeries, practices that took two thousand years to be repeated. His writings were the basis of medical studies well into the Middle Ages.

INSTRUMENTS
The Greek surgical instruments -in the picture-, were used until the times of the Roman Empire.

Milestones in Ancient Medicine

1 2500 BC
The Egyptian Hesy-Ra was the first physician and dentist known. Ebers Papyrus was the first compilation of remedies (Egypt, 1500 BC).

2 2000 BC
In Babylonian, texts were written for medical students on diagnostics and therapeutics. They were memorization exercises.

3 800 BC
In the *Iliad*, Homer includes explanations on techniques to treat war wounds. A century later, the first medical school was founded.

4 300 BC
Erasistratus and Herophilus from Chalcedon founded the the first scientific medical school in Alexandria. Their legacy includes anaesthesia and ophthalmology.

PHARMACOPOEIA
Remedies with medicinal properties were preserved in papyri including their preparation.

WIZARD-PHYSICIAN
He was in charge of performing magic spells needed to make more effective the medical treatment.

Birth of a Science

From the sixth century BC, Greek medicine began to attribute the causes of diseases to a natural origin, stripping them of religious practices. It emphasized the detailed observation of symptoms and the analysis of the clinical history of the patients. Its leading figure was Hippocrates (460 BC – c. 370 BC), creator of the famous Hippocratic oath.

CONVALESCENCE
Until the nineteenth century anaesthesia was not applied to patients. The Egyptians used different types of painkillers and drugs.

Hippocrates Practicing Medicine. In this carving of the fifth century BC, the Greek physician is depicted curing a woman.

Science in China

An archaeological discovery revealed that 4,000 years ago in China people already ate pasta, an example which illustrates the enormous technological and scientific advancement of a civilization which achieved enormous progress in chemistry, medicine and astronomy.

Pioneers

More than 4,000 years ago, silk was made in China. Over the centuries, this civilization also began making porcelain (17 century BC) and casting iron (4th century BC). The Chinese were, in turn, the inventors of paper (first century), printing (eight century, much earlier than Europe) and steelmaking, which made possible the construction of suspension bridges already in the sixth century, and the development of animal traction harnesses.

MERIDIAN LINES
Acupuncture identifies thirteen large interconnected channels or meridians associated to vital organs.

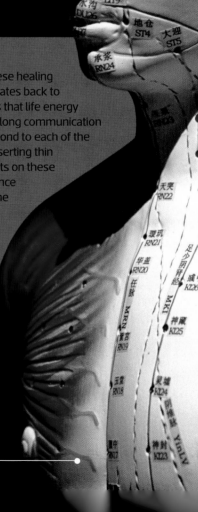

Advances
The different advances of Chinese scientists quickly obtained a practical application.

1 Astronomy
They manufactured equipment for observing the cosmos and already in 400 BC they listed 29 comets in *the Book of Silk*.

2 Magnetism
Towards 200 BC, the compass was discovered for rites of divination. Since the year 1000 it has been used in navigation.

3 Chemistry
Taoist monks invented gunpowder in the 7th century, which was quickly applied for weapons.

4 Calculation
The Chinese abacus was perfected in the 10th century, allowing decimal and hexadecimal calculations

Acupuncture
It is the best known Chinese healing practices. Its oldest text dates back to 4,500 years ago. It states that life energy flows through our body along communication lines called *king* that respond to each of the body's vital organs. By inserting thin needles into specific points on these lines, they seek to rebalance the disrupted energy in the corresponding organ.

TESTED
The uses of acupuncture have been successful in cases of traumatisms, allergies and infections. It is also used

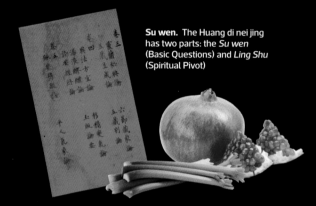

Handmade. Chinese physicians concocted by themselves the remedies they prescribed. In the picture, a 19th century apothecary.

Natural Way

In traditional Chinese medicine, the use of herbs, plants and flowers is fundamental both for healing and for disease prevention. So, they paid attention to the diets and the healing qualities of the plant world, establishing medicine branches such as herbal remedies such as aromatherapy.

Traditional Chinese Medicine

As old as its civilization, traditional Chinese medicine is based on the principles of energy balance, it proposes emotional, mental, spiritual and physical harmony, of which the forces of yin and yang are essential components. The best known of their treatment practices is acupuncture.

Su wen. The Huang di nei jing has two parts: the *Su wen* (Basic Questions) and *Ling Shu* (Spiritual Pivot)

INSERTION POINTS
According to the line, they communicate with the lungs, large intestine, small intestine, spleen-pancreas, heart, kidneys, bladder, cardiovascular system, gall bladder, stomach, liver, conception vessel, governing vessel and triple burner.

HUANG DI NEI JING
Written towards 2500 BC, it is the oldest work of Chinese medicine. It is a dialogue between the emperor and his doctor about diseases and treatments. There, among many other things, the healing properties of the pomegranate are mentioned, which is recommended for joint pain.

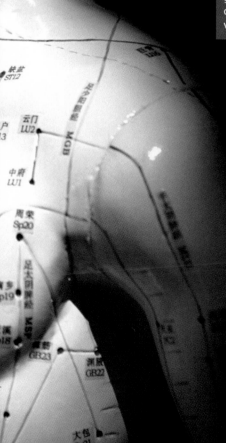

Zhang Heng

As a scientist, mathematician, astronomer, painter and writer, he was one of the leading figures of the Han dynasty. Known in the West as "The Leonardo of China," Zhang (78-139) designed a world map in which he located 2,500 stars and identified 124 constellations, he also calculated the celestial sphere to estimate the diameter of Earth and obtained the best approximation of the number pi until then: 3,162.

Versatile. Zhang, represented in this figure, also invented an earthquake detector.

Science in Ancient Greece

For more than five centuries, throughout the Classical and Hellenistic period, the Greek culture achieved decisive progress in every branch of knowledge, to the point that it eventually became the cradle of Western civilization.

The Greek Legacy

The critical thinking that was developed in Greece led to great advances for mankind, such as the birth of modern medicine by the hand of Hippocrates, the revolutionary mathematical advances by Pythagoras and Euclid, among others, or the new measurements and theories of the Greek astronomers. Many of the calculations and studies carried out in different areas of knowledge led to remarkable inventions, such as the lever or the pulley.

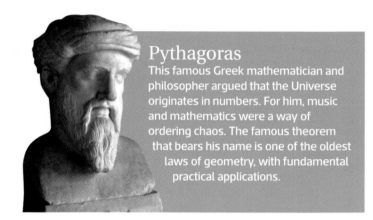

Pythagoras
This famous Greek mathematician and philosopher argued that the Universe originates in numbers. For him, music and mathematics were a way of ordering chaos. The famous theorem that bears his name is one of the oldest laws of geometry, with fundamental practical applications.

Astronomy

In Ancient Greece, there were remarkable astronomers, such as Eratosthenes of Cyrene, Aristarchus of Samos and Hipparchus of Nicaea, who calculated the proportions of the Earth, Sun and Moon and the distance between them, they began to catalog the stars and proposed the first heliocentric theories.

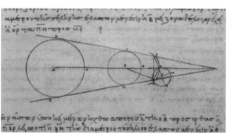

Measurements. Aristarchus' calculations relating to the proportions of the Sun, Earth and Moon.

Spherical. Diagram illustrating the calculation of the earth's circumference made by Eratosthenes.

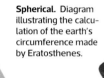

MEDICAL ADVANCES
In ancient Greece, splints and special stirrups for fractures were developed, similar to an external fixator, which facilitated welding of the bone.

Archimedes "moves" the World

One of the most extraordinary Greek scientists was Archimedes, who explained the physics of the lever with his phrase: "Give me a place to stand on, and I will move the Earth." He was also responsible for the first historical account of the pulley. It is believed that he used it to take a boat from the pier and led it to a dry dock.

THE CATAPULT
The Greeks invented several war machines. The most famous one is the catapult (4th century BC), developed to deal with the Carthaginians.

POSPARTUM
Hippocrates observed and analysed the possible mood disturbances of women after giving birth.

Medicine

The Greek medical school of Kos was the first in history that deserves to be described as scientific. We have inherited from it 30 treatises, based on the observation of the human body, in health and sickness, and on the experience and data collection. Its leading figure was the great physician Hippocrates (460-C -370 BC), considered the father of medicine because he definitively separated it from religion.

PEDIATRICS
Based on observation and experience, Hippocrates postulated that some childhood diseases became chronic.

HIPPOCRATES
He was the great figure of Greek medicine, the first physician who developed a rational system based on observation and experience.

The Greek Philosophers

Philosophy was the quintessential intellectual activity in classical Greece. The great Greek thinkers struggled to understand the world around them, including their own existence, always seeking explanations dictated by reason.

Loving Wisdom

The philosophers emerged in the Milesian School, in Asia Minor in the 6th century BC. The concerns of these thinkers exceeded the responses given so far by religion. They were not satisfied by the explanations provided by traditional myths about the origin of things, but they inquired into rational explanations to the questions that arose, and they promoted the investigation of natural phenomena. For their critical analysis of reality, in many cases they earned the enmity of the political and religious authorities of Ancient Greece.

ANAXIMANDER
He maintained that the source of all things was the "indefinite," a substance of divine origin.

EPICURUS
He argued that human pleasure was the absence of pain and related life to chance.

"The School of Athens"
This famous Renaissance painting by Raphael is an allegory of philosophy, and introduces the major thinkers of antiquity in the Academy of Plato. This philosopher founded his school in 387 BC, in Athens, to encourage the pursuit of knowledge about math, medicine, astronomy and rhetoric, among other subjects. Aristotle was his main disciple.

DIOGENES
He lived as a vagabond in Athens, turning extreme poverty into the virtue of knowledge.

PARMENIDES
He thought that the source of all things was fire. He stated: "Being and thinking are the same."

Thales of Miletus

He was the first known Greek philosopher. He learned geometry and astronomy in Egypt, and the legend says that he calculated the height of Jufu pyramid with a cane. When its shadow was equal to its length, he ordered measuring the shadow of the pyramid to get the height. Thus, he established the triangle proportionality theorem.

TRANSLATION

During the Renaissance, Lorenzo de Medici (picture) recreated the Platonic Academy in Florence. There, the texts of Plato were translated into Latin.

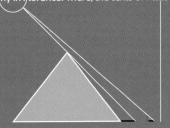

PTOLEMY
Dedicated to astronomy, he was the author of the geocentric organizational model: the Earth as the center of the universe.

ARISTOTLE
He possessed an encyclopaedic knowledge. He systematized all sciences, on which he wrote many treatises, especially about logic and biology, of which he is considered the founder.

PLOTINUS
He created the system of the Ones, which considers entirety as a whole governed by the metaphysical law of the unit.

PLATO
Disciple of Socrates, his prolific written word in dialogue form dealt with politics and the existence of two worlds, real and ideal.

SOCRATES
He held the principle that life is not worth it without analysis. He was executed for not recognizing the Athenian gods.

Astronomy in Ancient Times

Astronomy is considered the first of the natural sciences. It originated in mythological and religious practices of prehistory and the ancient civilizations perfected it gradually until it became a constant source of knowledge.

Result of the Need

Since the dawn of mankind, civilizations have developed their own ideas about the cosmos. In the sky, they looked for gods, divine messages, signs for their prophecies and references for their calendars. For the Egyptians, for example, the Milky Way was milk flowing from a heavenly cow. For the Mayan people, the universe was a flat square bounded by a lizard. And the primitive tribes of India believed that the Earth was a giant tray held by elephants on the shell of a turtle. Much of this knowledge from Ancient Times was refuted over time; other ideas, like the Mayan calendar, have striking similarities with current ones.

The Constellations

The origin of the constellations in Western culture dates back to Mesopotamia and reached the West through Greece, which explains why most of their names come from classical mythology. The latest constellations that were discovered bear names related to science and technology, or to the exotic wildlife discovered by Europeans in other continents.

THE PYRAMIDS AND THE STARS

For some, the alignment of the three stars of Orion's belt is related to the three pyramids of Giza (Egypt). Five millennia ago, Egyptians had already achieved the establishment of equinoxes with accuracy.

WESTERN ZODIAC
The 13 constellations that lie in the plane of the ecliptic- the apparent path line of the Sun as seen from Earth- are called zodiacal constellations and are the basis of astrology. Ptolemy was the first to list, by the second century, the 12 western zodiac signs.

Greek Knowledge

The Greek philosophers paid special attention to the movement of the heavenly bodies. For Plato, the universe was ruled by a soul or greater force, while for Aristotle believed in a system of concentric spheres that carried the planets to gravitate around the Earth.

Antikythera Mechanism. It dates back to 87 BC, it is a sophisticated gear mechanism to calculate the position of the sun.

Chinese Astronomy

More ancient than, and very different from the one of the Western world, Chinese astronomy was primarily aimed at the calculation time. Initially, it established that the Earth was in a plane and the sky in another (about 40,000 km), in which the Sun moved. The sky was divided into four regions and these into 28 "mansions," which would be equivalent to Western constellations.

For the first time in 185 AD, Chinese astronomers registered the first known supernova in history.

Different Cultures

In Ancient Times, each culture developed very different constellations. In fact, their names often do not coincide with the names of the constellations, though Scorpio is recognized by Mesopotamia, Greece, Rome, Mesoamerica and Oceania.

SCORPIO
In Roman mythology, Orion and Scorpio are intimately linked. Scorpio killed the handsome and giant hunter.

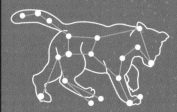

THE BIG DIPPER
The bear in this constellation is unusual in that it has a long tail. The drawings rarely match their names.

THE CENTAUR
It is a creature from Greek mythology, half man, half horse. He joined Orion in his eventful journey to see again.

Mintaka
Alnilam
Alnitak

TIME GUIDE
The Egyptians were guided by the stars to be able to tell the night hours. Later, the Greeks established the same hours for the day and night based on the equinoxes.

Orion. Representation of one of the most recognizable constellations, visible from both hemispheres.

Pre-Columbian Science

Before the arrival of the Spanish people in America, pre-Columbian cultures had reached different scientific achievements, such as using the number zero in mathematics or the accuracy of Mayan calendars.

Stargazing

As it happened in other agricultural cultures, such as the Egyptian or Mesopotamian ones, the early civilizations of pre-Columbian America paid special attention to the observation of the stars so as to predict the times of year for planting and harvest. in this field, the Mayan civilization shone above others, like the Aztecs or the Incas, developing calendars with admirable precision.

THE METHOD

To set the path of the stars, the priests would sit on top of a temple and watch the horizon with a stick attached to the ground. They measured the passage of the Sun through its zenith when the stick did not cast its shadow.

Mayan Astronomy

This Mesoamerican culture reached the highest astronomical and scientific development of all pre-Columbian America. The Mayans paid special attention to the Sun, following the path of said star, and to the observation of the Milky Way, known by them as the *World Tree* and represented by a ceiba tree.

Natural Medicine

In the pre-Columbian civilizations of America, medicine was related to religion. In the main cultures, healers employed prayers and sacrifices, as well as natural remedies, to heal the sick. The Incas, for example, had physicians who were specialists in plants, healers to which magical powers were attributed and surgeons who treated fractures and wounds.

Codex de la Cruz-Badiano. Latin translation of the first Aztec treatise describing the healing properties of some plants.

Inca Architecture

The Inca constructions are the best example of the scientific and cultural progress of these people. Major fortresses, as Machu Picchu, canals and aqueducts for irrigation, paved roads and bridges testify to this. They were also good astronomers and they created their own accounting system -*quipu*- based on strings which were knotted.

Inca roadways. Usually, the roads were a straight line of assembled rocks, with stone steps on slopes.

COMMENTS
This building contains a cylindrical tower that houses a small vaulted chamber. From there, the Mayas performed astronomic observations.

Math Teachers

The Mayan mathematical symbols were three: one stylized shell for zero, a dot for one and a stripe for five. Numbers were arranged vertically.

The mathematics were incorporated into the calendar in the so-called Long Count calculation, which consisted in the accumulation of five types of cycles of time (kin, uinal, tun, katun, baktun), with the numeral coefficients (number of days) by which they needed to be multiplied.

POSITIONAL VALUES

x	144.000	Baktun
x	7.200	Katun
x	360	Tun
x	20	Uinal
x	1	Kin

0	1	4	5	11	19	20	126	1.092	36.102	1.368.080	x (times)	days

Observatory. Mayan building, known as El Caracol, located in the city of Chichen Itza, Yucatan (Mexico).

Aztec Calendar

The Aztecs relied on two types of calendars, which they used to optimize and systematize their economic production cycles and to regulate religious activities. The civil or solar calendar provided time coordinates for planting and harvesting. The mystical or sacred calendar, however, was used to make predictions, horoscopes and to point out which were the luckiest days. The first one was divided into 365 days, and the second one, in 260.

The First Scientists

Although we know of the existence of great scientists in ancient civilizations, such as the Sumerian or Babylonian, we get to know in detail the first big names in science as from Classical Greece.

Children of Philosophy

The first people to use reason and experience to seek an explanation to the phenomena of nature were the pre-Socratic philosophers, -Thales, Heraclitus and Pythagoras, among others- who were followed the great thinkers of Athens, -Socrates, Plato, Aristotle-, the scientists from the Alexandrian period -Archimedes, Aristarchus, Hipparchus, Euclid, Eratosthenes, etc.- and later, others such as Ptolemy or Galen. They all were characterized by studying multiple disciplines.

Alexandria, Beacon of Knowledge

This city of Hellenistic Egypt succeeded Athens as the main center of knowledge in Ancient Times. Its famous library was located within a cultural institution called Museum. Tradition says that all the books that came into town were seized and duplicated by copyists.

ARCHIMEDES
287-212 BC
Mathematician, physicist, astronomer and inventor, he discovered the principle which states that a body immersed in a fluid experiences an up-thrust equal to the weight of the fluid displaced.

HIPPARCHUS
190-120 BC
Among his many achievements in astronomy, mathematics and geography, he is the prominent creator of the first catalog of stars. Besides, he is considered the inventor of trigonometry.

ARISTARCHUS
310-213 BC
Greek astronomer and mathematician, he was the first to propose a heliocentric model of the solar system. He made very accurate calculations of the distances between the Earth, Sun and Moon.

Masters of Eastern Science

In the ancient Chinese science, there were remarkable pioneers such as, Cai Lun (50–121), inventor of paper; the astronomer and mathematician Zhang Heng (78–139); and the mathematician Zu Chongzhi (429–500), who came closer than anyone calculating the value of pi. In India, the cradle of great mathematicians, Pingala created a binary number system in the 3rd century BC.

PIONEER
Hypatia of Alexandria (370–415) was the first scientist woman of whom we are aware. She studied mathematics, astronomy, philosophy and mechanics.

Heron of Alexandria (c. 10-70)

This revolutionary mathematician and engineer surprised his contemporaries with implausible inventions in which he reflected his mastery of mechanics, hydraulics and pneumatics. The two most prominent inventions were the aeolipile, considered the first steam engine, and Heron's fountain, a hydraulic machine that propelled water jets.

Aeolipile. It was the first machine capable of transforming thermal energy into mechanical.

GALEN
130-200
Together with Hippocrates, he was the great figure of ancient medicine. Great expert in anatomy, Galen studied in Alexandria before moving to Rome where he was the physician of several emperors.

PTOLEMY
C. 100 – C. 170
He elaborated the geocentric theory that prevailed in Ancient Times by which the Earth was the center of the universe and all the planets and stars revolved around in circular orbits.

EUCLID
C. 325 BC – C. 265 BC
He is considered the father of geometry. His extensive work *The Elements* is a very comprehensive collection of the mathematical knowledge of the time, and it was in force until the 19th century.

Chapter 2

Science in the Middle and Modern Ages

During the Middle Ages, even though the first universities were born, science lived a period of less commotion. Alchemy, which combined many disciplines, became very important in Europe, until it later became Chemistry. China and the Islamic Empire were the civilizations with the larger scientific development. Standing out are the contributions of the Arab world in mathematics and medicine, with characters like Al-Juarissmi or Avicena, whose ideas and advances spread widely outside of the Islamic world. Chinese technological potential, which was hardly shown outside its borders, was able to be seen in other countries during the famous maritime expeditions of Zheng He.

By the end of the Middle Ages and during the entire Modern Age, necessary changes were produced for the definite take off of modern science. Renaissance ideas eased this transition towards the scientific Revolution, embedded in the figures of Copernicus, Galileo and Kepler. At the end of the 17th century, Isaac Newton set the foundations of modern science with his discoveries in classical mechanics (the three laws of motion and the universal gravitation law) and in optics (nature of white light), besides being the inventor of the first reflection telescope and having developed infinitesimal calculus in mathematics.

Science in Medieval Islam

The Islamic Empire experienced a great development during the Middle Ages all along its vast territory. Cities were the great sources of scientific activity, through the public schools that they opened in them.

Creators of Algebra

It is not by chance that terms such as "algebra" and "algorithm" come from the Arabs. During the medieval period, the Islamic world became the main scientific focal point in the world. Since the 12th century, characters like mathematician and astronomer Al-Khwarismi or the doctor and philosopher Avicenna, continued the road started by the Greek philosophers more than a millennium before. They spread the decimal numerical system in Arab numbers, they developed algebra, they used – just like in India – irrational numbers, zero and negatives, they widened the Indian system of decimals and fractions, and they achieved advancement in the theory of numbers.

Bayt al-Hikma, the House of Wisdom

This is the name by which an official school is known, founded in Baghdad, the capital of the Abbasid caliphate, in the 9th century. It was finished under the ruling of Al-Ma'mun caliphate (813 – 833) and became one of the most important mathematics centers of the Arab world. It was destroyed during the Mongol invasion to Baghdad in the year 1258.

Hydraulic Mechanics

Arab science had a mostly experimental and technical character. The great development that Mechanics achieved, stayed reflected in the construction of hydraulic works – diversion dams, acequias (water conduits), waterwheels – meant to improve agricultural activity.

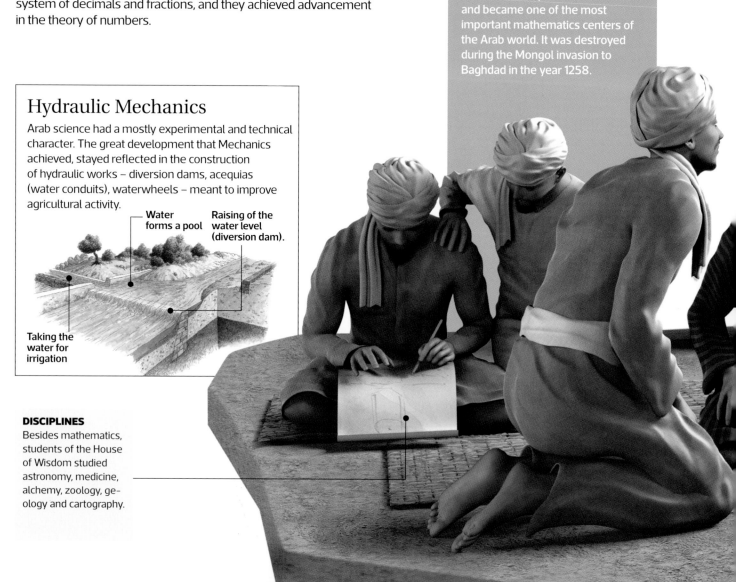

Water forms a pool

Raising of the water level (diversion dam).

Taking the water for irrigation

DISCIPLINES
Besides mathematics, students of the House of Wisdom studied astronomy, medicine, alchemy, zoology, geology and cartography.

Avicenna, Man of Science

Persian doctor, naturalist and philosopher, Avicenna (980 – 1037) was an official in the court of Baghdad. He left behind around two hundred works, most of them dedicated to scientific studies. Among them, the *Canon of Medicine* stands out, which was translated to Latin by Gerardo de Cremona in the 12th century and had a great diffusion in all Europe.

ALCHEMIST
Abu Ibn Sina, called Avicenna, doing one of his experiments about alchemy opposites with an eagle and a frog.

Advances in Astronomy

Creation of calendars, celestial maps and instruments like the astrolabe, got better due to the observations and calculations of the Islam astronomers on the equinoxes and solar and lunar eclipses. In the year 1000, Al-Biruni calculated the radius of the Earth with an error of only 7 km.

Astrolabe. Model of this navigation instrument from the 9th century.

LIBRARY
The House of Wisdom had great translators and a notable library with works of Galen, Hippocrates, Plato, Aristotle...

AL-KHWARISMI
One of the most prominent members of the Bayt al-Hikma center was Al-Khwarismi, considered the father of algebra.

The First Universities

Beginning in 1150, parochial, cathedral and monastic schools of the Late Middle Ages in Europe were substituted by universities, institutions created by the Church to keep knowledge under control, which moved freely in the cities.

The New Teaching

During the Middle Ages, new educational practices established in the cities. The first universities came from western Europe in the 12th century, as corporations of teachers and students. The first instance was the Preparatory Arts School, where they taught the *trivium* and the *quadrivium*, typical organization of contents of Ancient times. The first one covered the "humanist" knowledge: grammar, dialectics and rhetoric, and the second one the "realizts": arithmetic, geometry, astronomy and music. After finishing with these subjects, they could go on with their studies in Canon or Civil Law, medicine or theology.

Oxford and Cambridge

Oxford University (1096) appeared due to the royal restriction for British people to attend in Paris. Cambridge University (1209) was a division of it: a group of professors retired because of differences with authorities.

Specialized Studies

Some universities were specialized. The Salernitana Medical School (Italy), with roots in the 9th century, stood out in medicine; and the Montpellier University (France), created in 1088, housed the first Law studies.

LEVELS
Students, who used to live in the nearby collective dormitories (schools), could graduate as bachelor, magister or doctor.

Anatomy. In the Early Middle Ages anatomy began to use human corpses instead of animals like the pig.

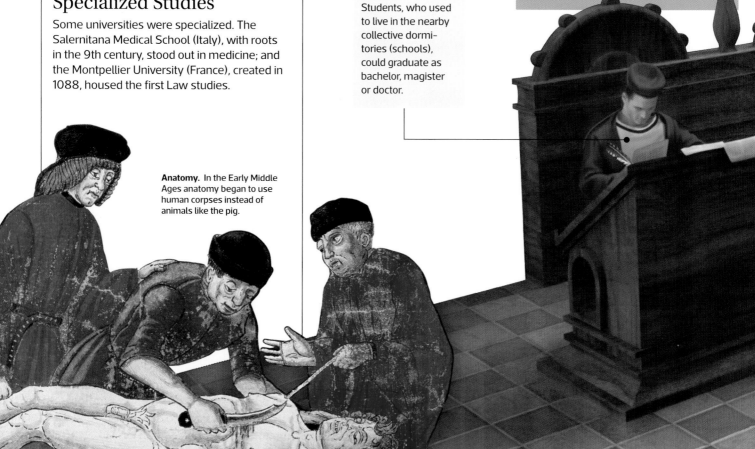

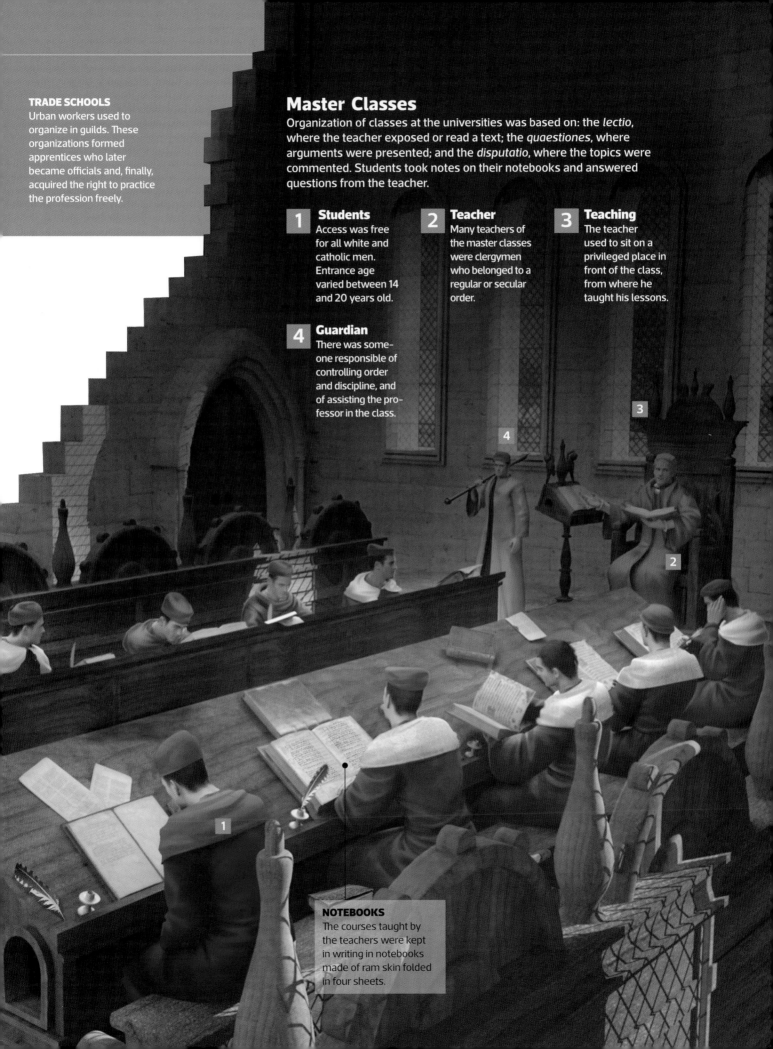

TRADE SCHOOLS
Urban workers used to organize in guilds. These organizations formed apprentices who later became officials and, finally, acquired the right to practice the profession freely.

Master Classes
Organization of classes at the universities was based on: the *lectio*, where the teacher exposed or read a text; the *quaestiones*, where arguments were presented; and the *disputatio*, where the topics were commented. Students took notes on their notebooks and answered questions from the teacher.

1 Students
Access was free for all white and catholic men. Entrance age varied between 14 and 20 years old.

2 Teacher
Many teachers of the master classes were clergymen who belonged to a regular or secular order.

3 Teaching
The teacher used to sit on a privileged place in front of the class, from where he taught his lessons.

4 Guardian
There was someone responsible of controlling order and discipline, and of assisting the professor in the class.

NOTEBOOKS
The courses taught by the teachers were kept in writing in notebooks made of ram skin folded in four sheets.

Medieval Alchemy

Wrapped in a halo of mystery, alchemy, whose origin goes back to Ancient China, Egypt and Arabia, recovered popularity in Europe during the Middle Ages. Its practitioners were a mixture of scientists, philosophers and mystics.

Philosophical Chemistry

Hermetic, mysterious and full of symbolisms, alchemy had the desire for human perfection and the search for a substance – the "philosopher's stone" – which would be able to transmute basic metals into gold and also to create an immortality elixir. It never reached its objectives, since transmutation from one atom to another was not accomplished until 1919, thanks to the use of physical methods. However, it developed devices and procedures like distillation and purification of metals, which later were used by modern chemistry and metallurgy laboratories.

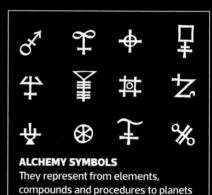

ALCHEMY SYMBOLS
They represent from elements, compounds and procedures to planets and periods of time.

READINGS
Many of the Arab alchemy works were translated to Latin beginning on the 12th century. Yabir ibn Hayyan, known as Geber, was the most important Arab alchemist.

APPRENTICE
The assistant to the alchemist gets a glass retort with which he is trying to distil an essence close to the furnace. Distillation with stills allowed, for example, isolating the "spirit" of the wine: ethylic alcohol.

PARACELSUS (1493-1541)

Swiss alchemist, doctor and astrologer. He condemned the medical practice of his time and postulated that diseases were not curable with chemical remedies.

JOHN DEE (1527-1608)

Mathematician, astronomer and counselor of Queen Elizabeth I of England, this alchemist committed himself both to science as to magic, astrology and Hermetic philosophy.

ATHANOR FURNACE

Alchemical fusion oven. It had a solid external cover and an interior full of ashes that covered the "philosophical egg" or glass sphere where the matter that needed to be kept hot was located.

The Philosopher's Stone

Assumed substance that, according to alchemists, was capable of achieving transmutation into gold, immortality (by means of the universal panacea) and omniscience or total knowledge of the past and the future. The starting point to obtain the miraculous substance was iron pyrite or iron disulfide.

THE ALCHEMIST

Using a bellow, he stokes the fire next to the athanor or "philosopher's oven." It was important to maintain a uniform temperature that would allow heating substances for long period of time.

PRESS

It was an indispensable instrument in the alchemy workshop. It was used to extract oils or essences by pressing of seeds, fruit or other parts of plants.

Science in the Renaissance

The curiosity of the Renaissance scientists lead them to substitute speculative medieval science for experimental science, motivating the advancement of astronomy, mathematics, physics, chemistry, anatomy and medicine.

Copernican Revolution

Polish astronomer Nicolaus Copernicus (1473 - 1543) was one of the great protagonists of Renaissance science. When he published his work *The Revolution of Celestial Bodies* (*De revolutionibus orbium coelestium*) in 1543, he not only shook up classic astronomy. He also stated a new idea about the Universe: the Sun was the center of the planetary system, and not the Earth, as it was affirmed since the times of astronomer Ptolemy (2nd Century). The Copernican theory shook the foundations of science and also of the Catholic Church, who did not accept the new conception of the world.

PTOLEMY AND GEOCENTRISM
The left side of the illustration represents the model promoted by Ptolemy, according to which the Earth was still while the Sun, the Moon and the five planets known in those times circled around it.

An Unrepeatable Genius

Painter, architect, physicist, botanic, doctor, writer... Leonardo da Vinci (1452-1519), another one of the characters of the Renaissance, was ahead of his time. His multifaceted spirit covered all the branches of knowledge. Supported by his privileged gift for drawing, he made sublime anatomy studies and invented all kinds of machines.

Ornithopter. One of the machines invented by Leonardo.

Advancement of Medicine

Medicine went through a key impulse in the Renaissance, especially in the fields of anatomy, with important works by Leonardo and Andres Vesalio, and of surgery, thanks to Ambrosio Pare and Paracelso, who applied the new methods giving priority to diagnostics, before intervention. Miguel Servet studied the flow of blood in the lungs.

Canon of proportions. The notable anatomic study of the human body by Leonardo.

Heliocentric Model

Copernicus argued that a sphere moved on a circular orbit with no beginning or end. Since the universe and all celestial bodies are spherical, their movements should also be circular and uniform. In the Ptolemaic system, the circuit of the planets was irregular. Copernicus then deduced that if the movements of the planets appeared as irregular to our sight, it was because the Earth was not the center of the universe.

CELESTIAL ATLAS

In the right half of the illustration, a fragment of *The Copernican system*, an etching of the *Macrocosmic Harmony atlas* (Andreas Cellarius, 1660).

Introducer of Empiricism

Francis Bacon (1561 - 1626) made experience the starting point of all knowledge. To him, science was the indispensable instrument to decipher and rule over the secrets of nature. Thus, his motto: "knowledge is power," which had a decisive influence on empiricism.

Portrait of Bacon from the 18th century. His figure incarnated the last stage of the Renaissance.

The Scientific Revolution

The development of the experimental method and the new way of thinking the world based more on the discovery of its laws that in the compliance of divine plans, was translated in a revolutionary advancement of science in the 17th century.

First Steps of Modern Science

The publishing in 543 of two key works for history of science – *De revolutionibus orbium coelestium*, where Copernicus exposed his heliocentric theory, and De humani corporis fabrica, the formidable anatomy treatise of Andres Vesalio – meant the beginning of a revolutionary era that developed all its splendor along the 12th century. Scientists betted for the experimental method and for mathematics as a universal language, in an era full of great inventions, like the microscope and the telescope, which allowed knowing the world better, from cells to the Universe.

REGULATOR
It is the declination axis for the adjustments.

VIRTUALITY
Here the internal lens gets a virtual image.

OBJECTIVE
It consists in a system of convergent lenses.

REALITY
In this point, another lens provides the real and inverted image.

THE TELESCOPE
Galileo created this divergent ocular lens in 1609, which preceded Newton's reflector telescope (1671). It allowed watching enlarged images of distant objects. With it, he studied the Moon, Jupiter and the stars.

OCULAR
Divergent lenses system. It acts as a magnifier.

TVBVM·OPTICVM·VIDES·GALILAEII·INVENTVM·ET·OPVS.QVO·SOLIS·MACVLAS,
ET·EXTIMOS·LVNAE·MONTES·ET·IOVIS·SATELLITES,ET·NOVAM·QVASI
RERVM·VNIVERSITATE·PRIMVS·DISPEXIT·A.MDCIX.

Prominent Characters

The scientific and technical revolution of the 17th century was propelled by some names that have entered history. Their contributions are many. Here we show some of the most significant ones.

GALILEO GALILEI
Italian astronomer and physicist (1564 - 1642), he is located at the top of the great researchers of the 12th century. Pioneer of modern mechanics, he registered the first divergent ocular lens (telescope).

JOHANNES KEPLER
German astronomer and mathematician (1571 - 1630). He formulated the laws that describe the movement of the planets in their orbits.

And Yet, It Moves

Accused by the Inquisition in 1633, Galileo retracted of his astronomical statements being threatened of dying burned alive. Legend says that Galileo muttered the words "Eppur si muove" ("And yet, it moves"), referring to the movement of the Earth around the Sun.

BLOOD FLOWS
William Harvey proved that an obstruction of a vein in the arm interrupts the flow of blood to the elbow and not to the wrist, as it was believed.

THE MICROSCOPE
It was invented during the middle of the 17th century by Dutch optician Anton van Leeuwenhoek (1632 – 1723). Robert Hooke built this compound model in 1670.

OCULAR
Second lenses system.

CONDENSER
Oil lamp and water flask.

SCREW
Focus regulator.

OBJECTIVE
Short focal distance lens.

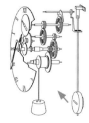

BRACE
Here is where the specimen is placed.

Experimental Science

Barometer and thermometer
In 1643, Torricelli discovered and determined the value of atmospheric pressure, a discovery that allowed him to invent the barometer and the thermometer.

Mercury

Pendulum clock
Huygens two precise oscillators to clock making: the pendulum and the flywheel. The first one moved by the action of gravity and regulated the gears of the clock.

The vacuum effect
Physicist Otto von Guericke joined two hemispheres and made a vacuum in them. The force of atmospheric pressure prevents them from being separated.

EVANGELISTA TORRICELLI
Italian physicist and mathematician (1608 – 1647). He formulated the law of atmospheric pressure and the one of spilling of liquids.

BLAISE PASCAL
French mathematician and philosopher (1623 – 1662). He initiated mechanical calculus and established principles about fluids.

CHRISTIAAN HUYGENS
Dutch mathematician, physicist and astronomer (1629 – 1695). He studied the pendulum and explained reflection and diffraction.

ROBERT HOOKE
British astronomer and mathematician (1635 – 1703). He perfected the microscope, observing the cells of vegetable tissues.

ISAAC NEWTON
British scientist (1642 – 1727). He formulated the universal gravitational law and created the reflection telescope. Author of *Optics*.

Newton and Classical Physics

This British physicist and mathematician incorporated the new philosophy to understand the world developed by the scientific revolution, initiated in the last stage of the Renaissance, and which was based on three key points: observation, experimentation and reasoning.

Model of Physics

The first one that systematized modern physics was Isaac Newton, creator of classical mechanics, which was valid until Einstein. In his work *Mathematical principles of natural philosophy* (1687), he formulated the binomial theorem; he created the Method of fluxions and conceived the idea of universal gravitation. His research on optics led him to establish the composition of white light and the theory of colors. At the same time, he formulated the basic laws of motion that carry his name.

WHITE SCREEN
On the white surface prepared by Newton, the seven colors spectrum is formed: red, orange, yellow, green, blue, indigo and violet.

Universal Gravitation

Newton formulated the famous law of universal gravitation. In it, he established that gravitational force of attraction between two masses of the Universe is: a) directly proportional to the product of their masses (that is why the Earth applies more attraction than the Moon); b) inversely proportional to the square of the distance between them (as farther we are from the Earth, less is the gravity).

Inspiration. The legend says that the fall of an apple inspired Newton.

Newton's Laws

The British physicist came up with three basic principles to answer all questions related with general mechanics and with motion of bodies in particular.

1 Law of inertia
An object stays at rest or in motion unless external forces act upon it.

2 Law of force
Acceleration of a body is directly proportional to the net force acing upon it and inversely proportional to its mass.

3 Law of action and reaction
When an object exerts force onto another, the second object exerts a counterpart force in the opposite direction back onto the first object.

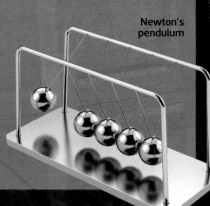

Newton's pendulum

The Royal Society

For more than two decades, from 1704 until his death in 1727, Isaac Newton presided over the Royal Society in London, where he exposed many of his theories in front of the most brilliant scientists of that time. Founded in 1660, this prestigious scientific society is still fulfilling the function of Academy of Sciences of the United Kingdom.

Meeting. Members of the Royal Society with Newton in the front, sitting on a chair.

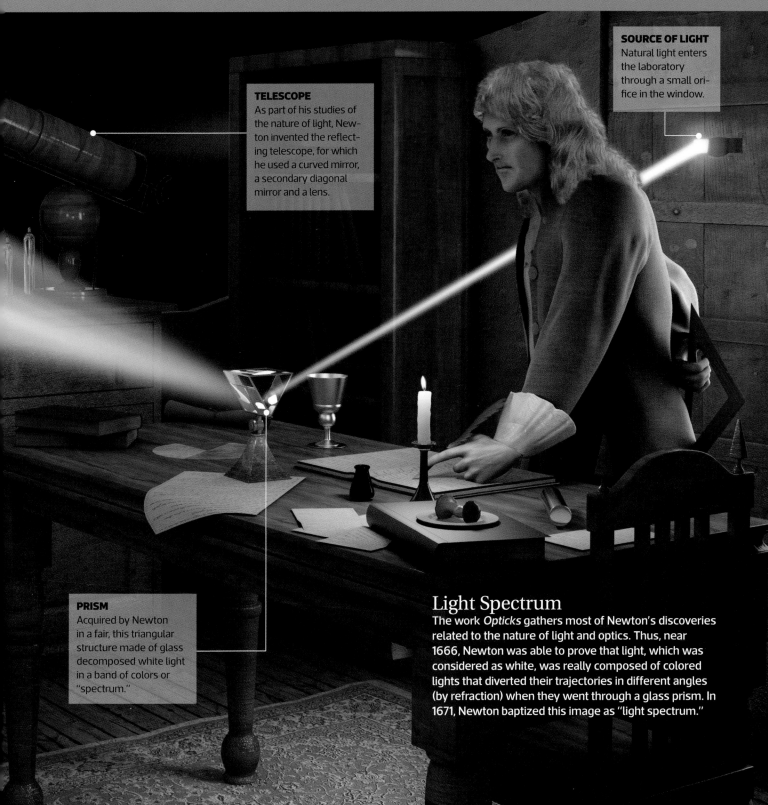

SOURCE OF LIGHT
Natural light enters the laboratory through a small orifice in the window.

TELESCOPE
As part of his studies of the nature of light, Newton invented the reflecting telescope, for which he used a curved mirror, a secondary diagonal mirror and a lens.

PRISM
Acquired by Newton in a fair, this triangular structure made of glass decomposed white light in a band of colors or "spectrum."

Light Spectrum

The work *Opticks* gathers most of Newton's discoveries related to the nature of light and optics. Thus, near 1666, Newton was able to prove that light, which was considered as white, was really composed of colored lights that diverted their trajectories in different angles (by refraction) when they went through a glass prism. In 1671, Newton baptized this image as "light spectrum."

Scientific Expeditions

The spirit of the Enlightenment and the Encyclopedia woke up the urge for knowledge of many countries, which in the 18th century organized numerous expeditions to collect scientific information about the colonies and to define the cartography of the new territories.

Thirst for Knowledge

In the Age of Enlightenment, the colonizing adventures of conquerors and missionaries opened the way to scientific expeditions. The great European powers organized various trips, perfectly programmed, in which they had scientists, naturalists, doctors and, most of all, skillful artists that captured whatever they saw on their way in laborious drawings. France sent Bouganville, La Condamine and La Pérouse; Hispanic monarchy organized several botanical expeditions and the ambitious trip of Malaspina for its possessions; and England had the famous captain James Cook.

Documentation

Humboldt brought 60,000 species of vegetables and some of animals from his trip to South America, besides accurately drawing many others. He collected the information in his work *Travel to the Equinoctial Regions of the New Continent*.

Toucan. It was one of the tropical species that Humboldt collected.

Alexander von Humboldt

Great German explorer and scientist, considered the father of modern geography, Humboldt made a great trip along Frenchman Aimé Bonpland, which allowed him to go over the Spanish colonies in America between 1799 and 1804. The result was a colossal work of 30 volumes written along 20 years.

Humboldt's Contributions

Besides creating file cards of botany and zoology, his interest focused on so varied fields like history, geography, botany, cartography, vulcanology or social sciences. He dedicated himself to studying, among other topics:

1 Oceans
He studied the oceanic current of the western coast of South America that currently bears his name.

2 Climate
He created a new system to represent temperatures (in the form of isobars and isotherms).

3 Conditions
He made comparative studies between climate and ecological conditions of a delimited territory.

4 Volcanoes
He got conclusions about volcanic activity and its relationship with Earth's crust.

JAMES COOK

He made three expeditions with an astronomical and cartographic character around the Pacific. In the last one he discovered the Sandwich Islands (Hawaii), where he was murdered.

Bougainville's Trip

Louis-Antoine de Bougainville (1729-1811) was the first French sailor that completed a trip around the world (1766-1769), accompanied by naturalists and astronomers. During his trip he explored the Magellan Strait – image -, collecting very valuable information about the region.

Malaspina Expedition

For five years (1789 - 1794), Lieutenant Alessandro Malaspina and his friend José de Bustamante onboard two corvettes commanded a colossal political – scientific expedition financed by Hispanic monarchy. Three were the main objectives: cartographic mapping of the sailed coasts, socio political reports of the colonies, and analysis of the fauna, flora, and mineralogy of the visited territories.

Alaska
Nootka
Acapulco
Cadiz
Manila
Tonga
Lima
Port Jackson
To Cadiz
Santiago
Montevideo
New Zealand
Falkland Islands

Malaspina. His expedition was a success, but he did not receive the recognition he deserved.

Great route. Malaspina and Bustamante departed from Cadiz (Spain) and arrived at Australia after sailing along the entire western coast of America.

"Descubierta" and "Atrevida." The two corvettes of the Malaspina Expedition arriving at the Port of Palapa, in Philippines.

Darwin's Legacy

Charles Darwin's evolution theory (1809-1882), one of the greatest intellectual achievements in history, represents the fundamental roadmap that has allowed us to understand the dynamics of the species on Earth.

Natural Selection

Even though the idea that animals and plants were not always the same had already been proposed by other thinkers, like Anaximander in the 5th century BC, Darwin managed to conjugate observations and discoveries in a beautiful and consistent theory. The engine of evolution, as the father of modern biology stated, is a kind of an invisible force called "natural selection": the greater aptitude of certain members of a population, better adapted to their environment, to leave descendants with those same traits.

AUSTRALOPITHECUS
The precursor
This ape is one of the first links in the human evolution chain. It became extinct 1.5 million years ago. Its most notable trait was bipedalism.

HOMO HABILIS
Great leap
First link of the genre *Homo*, it went through important physiological changes compared to its ancestor.

BRAIN
Its brain grew a 44% compared to its ancestor (much more than the rest of the body).

OPPOSED THUMBS
With them it was able to manufacture the first stone utensils.

FREE HANDS
It was an advantageous consequence of bipedalism.

BIPEDISMO
It requires less energy to move and increases the field of vision, although it loses speed.

ANATOMY
Its bone density was lower than the one of its predecessors, but muscular mass was larger.

Human Evolution

Science has established bipedalism as the first stage in the road to hominization, which began at least four million years ago. Homo sapiens is the only surviving species.

4 million years ago

PARANTHROPUS

P. aethiopicus

A. ramidus → A. anamensis → A. afarensis → A. africanus

???

A. garhi

ARDIPITHECUS

AUSTRALOPITHECUS

HMS Beagle. This brigantine from the British Army made three great transoceanic journeys.

The Crucial Trip

Between 1831 and 1836, Darwin traveled throughout South America, Africa and Oceania onboard the *HMS Beagle*. The enormous amount of information about the fauna, flora, geology and human customs of half the world, collected and written in his diary along five years, were essential to later publish his theories in The origin of species in 1859.

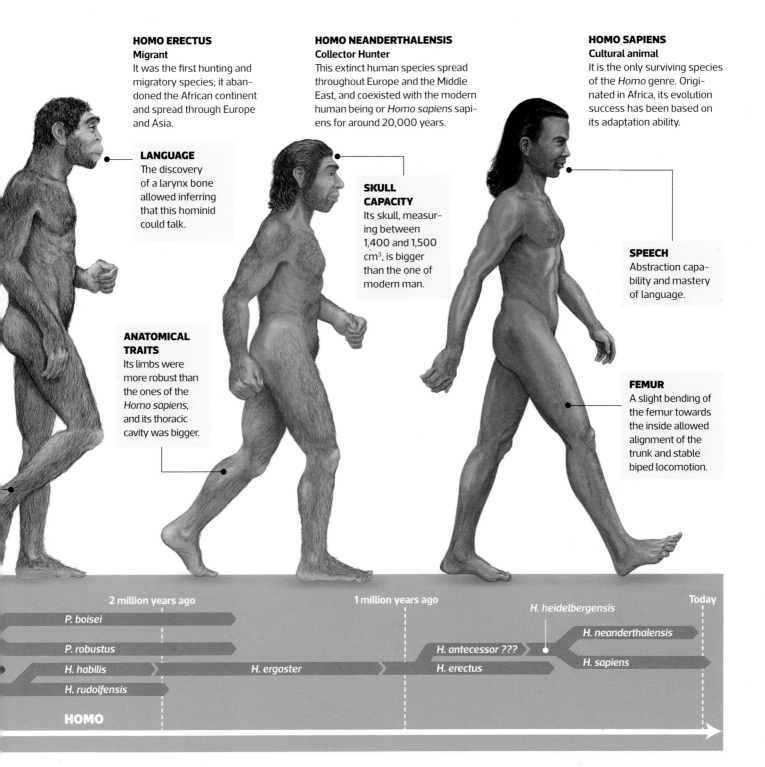

HOMO ERECTUS
Migrant
It was the first hunting and migratory species; it abandoned the African continent and spread through Europe and Asia.

HOMO NEANDERTHALENSIS
Collector Hunter
This extinct human species spread throughout Europe and the Middle East, and coexisted with the modern human being or *Homo sapiens* sapiens for around 20,000 years.

HOMO SAPIENS
Cultural animal
It is the only surviving species of the *Homo* genre. Originated in Africa, its evolution success has been based on its adaptation ability.

LANGUAGE
The discovery of a larynx bone allowed inferring that this hominid could talk.

SKULL CAPACITY
Its skull, measuring between 1,400 and 1,500 cm^3, is bigger than the one of modern man.

SPEECH
Abstraction capability and mastery of language.

ANATOMICAL TRAITS
Its limbs were more robust than the ones of the *Homo sapiens*, and its thoracic cavity was bigger.

FEMUR
A slight bending of the femur towards the inside allowed alignment of the trunk and stable biped locomotion.

2 million years ago — 1 million years ago — Today

H. heidelbergensis

P. boisei

P. robustus

H. antecessor ???

H. neanderthalensis

H. habilis — *H. ergaster* — *H. erectus* — *H. sapiens*

H. rudolfensis

HOMO

The Birth of Geology

Between the end of the 18th century and beginning of the 19th, geology appeared as the science in charge of studying the Earth. This is how the first theories that questioned the creationist version of the Bible about the origin of the planet appeared.

Neptunism and Plutonism

The first geological theories dealt with the origin of rocks. Abraham Werner (1749 – 1817) led the neptunist hypothesis, according to which would have been formed under the great ocean that covered the Earth after its creation. The antagonistic theory was plutonism, which attributed a volcanic origin to rocks. Its great leader was James Hutton (1726 – 1797), who stated that geological processes that transform the planet were uniform along history – uniformitarianism -. This theory implied that the Earth had an age of millions of years and not 6,000, as *Genesis* stated.

Charles Lyell. He is considered one of the founders of modern geology.

"Principles of Geology"

This book, published in three volumes between 1830 and 1833 was the great geology treatise of the 19th century. In it, British Charles Lyell (1797 - 1875) developed Hutton's ideas in a new theory called "uniformitarianism." For Lyell, all geological changes had been produced the same way and at the same rhythm than today. His theses influenced notably on the evolution theory that Darwin elaborated a few years later.

Models

Since the last years of the 18th century, geology went through a great rise as a consequence of the appearance of notable scholars, mainly British, German and French.

Abraham Werner

Considered father of mineralogy, stated that rocks originated in the bottom of the oceans, based on his research on stratus superposition.

James Hutton

In his work *Theory of the Earth* he exposed his ideas about slow and constant evolution of the planet (uniformitarianism). For many, he is the first modern geologist.

Geological Society of London

Founded in 1807, this institution was the first one dedicated specifically to studying geology, although in its beginning it was not formed by professional geologists, but for members of the Parliament, lawyers and clergymen. The reason was that the geological theories that were discussed in that time – catastrophism and uniformitarianism – had a great incidence on politics and theology.

Emblem of the institution. The Geological Society of London is the oldest in the world, and one of the most prestigious ones.

Great Advancements

During the last century, geology made great progress. In 1912, Alfred Wegener developed the continental drift theory; X-rays were used to analyze rocks and minerals since 1920; in 1950 exploration of the sea bottoms began, which allowed formulating the Tectonic Plates. In 1956, C. Patterson determined that the Earth was around 4,500 million years old using radiometric dating.

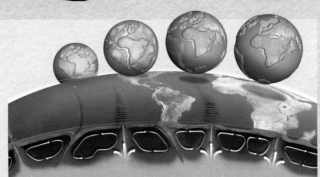

Mount Etna. One of the illustrations from *Principles of geology*, reference work by Charles Lyell.

William Smith
He was the first one to do chronological order of geological stratus by means of the study of fossils found in them.

Jean-Baptiste Lamarck
Founder of invertebrate paleontology, defended that the Earth has constant changes, although too slow.

Georges Cuvier
Great exponent of the catastrophic theories. He stated that the changes on the Earth were caused by violent punctual episodes, like earthquakes and volcanic eruptions.

The Social Sciences

Also known as human sciences, they group the scientific disciplines in charge of studying human activity and behavior in society, from different perspectives and in different eras. Most of them took off in the 18th century.

Knowing Social Reality

Despite the fact that the origin of history goes back to Ancient Greece, most of the social sciences had their first big impulse much later, during the Enlightenment. The desire for knowledge about man and human societies moved forward in the 19th century with the presence of social sciences in books, universities and scientific institutions, and consolidated in the 20th century thanks to figures like Sigmund Freud, Max Weber, Karl Marx, John Maynard Keynes and Claude Lévi-Strauss.

Are They Scientific?

Different than natural sciences, in social sciences the subject and object of study match, which has led to question its scientific character (Can a human being reach an objective knowledge of itself?). On the other hand, in most of the cases the hypotheses cannot be corroborated by laboratory experiments.

Evolution of Societies

Some of the most important social sciences have something in common: they study the development that societies have had throughout time, at different levels.

History

Its mission is reconstructing and studying the events that happened in societies of the past with the purpose of understanding better the present. It is, probably, the most ancient social discipline.

Archeology

It studies human societies throughout time based on material remains they have left behind. It got a new dimension in the 20th century thanks to technological advancements.

Demography

It analyzes human populations in quantitative and qualitative terms: evolution, structure, size...

Howard Carter. He was the most famous archaeologist of the 20th century.

Malthusian Catastrophe. Thomas Malthus, one of the pioneers of demography, predicted in 1803 that population would grow more than resources and it would become extinct.

Liberty Leading the People. This work of Delacroix symbolizes one of the key moments in history: The French Revolution.

Applied Social Sciences and Liberal Studies

There are numerous disciplines that are closely related with social sciences but apart from them. On one side, those that share the object of study but are integrated in the group of liberal arts for not considering their status as a science (philosophy, law, semiology, political science). And on the other side, the ones called "applied" (like pedagogy), which make use of social sciences for their development.

Machiavelli. Author of *The Prince* Niccolò Machiavelli was one of the fathers of political science.

Science and Social Interaction

The largest subgroup of social disciplines is formed by those dedicated to the study of interrelationships in human societies. These are the most significant sciences:

Anthropology
It searches for integral knowledge – biological and social – of human beings. For this, it uses other natural and social sciences.

Sociology
It studies the functioning and structure of societies under a scientific prism. It was created by French philosopher Auguste Comte.

Economy
It analyzes the way in which human beings and society manage production, distribution and consumption of its resources.

Human geography
It looks at societies from a spatial point of view: it studies the relationship between man and the environment where he lives.

Tribe. All peoples in the planet are study objects of human geography.

Claude Lévi-Strauss. One of the great characters of anthropology in the 20th century.

Cognitive Disciplines

Another subgroup of social sciences would be integrated by the disciplines that study the human cognitive system. Psychology and Linguistics are the main ones.

Psychology
It is the science that analyzes motivations, behavior and social conduct of the individuals. Sigmund Freud has been the great model of this discipline, which was linked to philosophy for a long time.

Linguistics
It studies language as a vehicle of expression of the human being. Its historical evolution, the way of learning, differences and similarities between languages, etc.

Ferdinand de Saussure. He is considered the founder of Linguistics.

Modern Chemistry

The publishing in 1789 of the *Elementary Treatise of Chemistry* by Antoine Lavoisier, a complete compendium of theories, formulations and technical descriptions, raised chemistry to the category of scientific discipline. In the 19th century, its advancement was meteoric.

Lavoisier's Legacy

Considered as father of modern chemistry, French scientist Antoine Lavoisier (1743 – 1794) achieved revolutionary advancements in his famous laboratory in Paris. He proved that matter is preserved in reactions, he revealed the composition of air and water, he described the function of oxygen in animal and vegetable respiration, and he studied alcoholic fermentation. He also defined the concept of chemical element and was the first one to use the scale as a scientific instrument.

PERIODIC TABLE
In 1869, Russian chemist Dmitri Mendeléiev published his famous periodic table, in which he ordered the elements according to their chemical properties.

Atomic Theory

Based on the atomic model formulated by John Dalton in 1808, the scientific community widely accepted that matter was formed, in the last instance, by indivisible and indestructible particles called atoms. Between the end of the 19th century and the beginning of the 20th, it was discovered that atoms were formed by protons, neutrons and electrons.

QUARK, A NEW LINK
In the 20th century, physics was in charge of proving that there are even more elemental particles: the quarks. And it has been theorized that energy filaments would be even smaller.

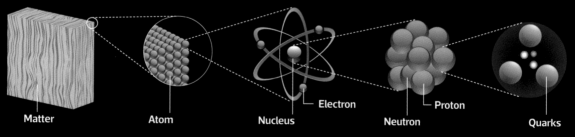

Matter   Atom   Nucleus   Electron   Neutron   Proton   Quarks

Chemistry Milestones from the 19th Century

Chemistry went through and era of great splendor during the 19th century, with the discovery of new elements, the development of organic chemistry and atomic theories, etc.

1802	1811	1813	1828	1867	1896
Gay-Lussac's Law This French chemist verified that, at a constant pressure, gasses expand proportionately to	**Avogadro's Law** Italian Amedeo Avogadro formulated the principle that allowed establishing the first differentiation between atoms and	**Chemical notation system** Swedish Jöns Berzelius creates the chemical notation system that is still current, based on the initial of each	**Organic chemistry** After obtaining urea from inorganic matter, Friedich Wöhler established the starting point of	**Dynamite** Notable Swedish chemist Alfred Nobel discovered the new explosive that replaced nitroglycerin for civil and military	**Radioactivity** Experimenting with uranium, Frenchman Henri Becquerel found a new property of matter that he would later call

Nobel Scientist

Marie Curie was the first person to receive two Nobel prizes. The one in Physics in 1903, together with her husband Pierre and Henri Becquerel, for her research about radiation phenomena, and the one in Chemistry in 1910 for the discovery of elements radium and polonium.

ACCIDENT
Pierre and Marie Curie formed an exceptional tandem in and out of the laboratory until, in 1906, he was run over by a carriage and died.

Madame Curie

French physicist and chemist of a Polish origin Marie Curie was one of the great scientific figures of the end of the 19th century and beginning of the 20th. As a result of her works about radioactivity, together with her husband Pierre, in 1898 she achieved isolating two new chemical elements: polonium, called that way in honor to Curie's country of origin, and radium.

The New Scientific Training

In Europe, the enlightenment school of thought that traveled throughout the continent in the 18th century and the extinction of the formative model of medieval scholastic propelled the birth of the modern universities. Science was institutionalized and centered on research.

Universities' Renovation

Beginning in the 19th century, scientific work started to develop mainly at universities. There were two main university models: the German, characterized for its dedication to research and autonomy of science facing the state, whose role was reserved to financing, and the French, based on government control of the study plans and discipline. The German pattern promoted by Wilhelm von Humboldt from his position as German Education Secretary, gave way to regulated research, while the French one left in the hands of private people.

Humboldt University in Berlin. Founded in 1810 by Wilhelm von Humboldt, was the main representative of the so called German model of university.

AUGUSTE COMTE
This French thinker (1798–1857) played an important role in the development of positivism, initiated by Henri de Saint-Simon.

The Laboratories
The appearance of research laboratories, provided with good equipment, implied the progressive development of an industry with a scientific foundation – factories of technology – which allowed abandoning traditional production.

Influence of Positivism

The positivist philosophy had a great weight in scientific development of the 19th century. Opposed to Romanticism, this tendency states that the only true knowledge is the one based on the scientific method, that is, the verified and objective data, without interference of other values and interests outside of science.

Professionalization of Science

The main changes that happened in the history of science during the 19th century turned it into an increasingly professionalized activity. The states realized its enormous potential power, especially in fields such as chemistry and physics, for which the scientific environment began being institutionalized in the more advanced countries.

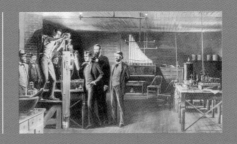

EDISON'S LABORATORY
American inventor Thomas Edison founded Menlo Park laboratory in 1876 (in the image), whose scientists obtained more than a thousand patents.

The new researchers
Students did their research in laboratories or seminaries at universities. Scientific team work was born and doctoral theses with a greater scientific value began getting published.

Scientific Dissemination

Improvement in education and the extraordinary development of science in the Modern Age led to a progressive approaching of it to the great public. Through dissemination, the complex scientific world started opening up to society with a more accessible language.

Science Widens Borders

In the 18th century society will begin to perceive scientific discoveries as a sign of progress. Dissemination of these advancements outside the scientific environment was manifested in the appearance of magazines and museum, and in exhibitions and conferences, among others. Many scientific terms were incorporated to the everyday language in this era.

THE BRITISH MUSEUM
It was created in 1753 with the purpose of preserving natural specimens and ethnographic material donated by naturalist Hans Sloane. Today it keeps only antiques.

THE ENCYCLOPÉDIE
French enlightened tried to collect and disseminate knowledge in this notable work from the 18th century.

CAMILLE FLAMMARION
This French astronomer (1842-1925) was one of the figures of the 19th century that made science popular with his works.

Modern Museums

The first great museums saw light in the 18th century. Until then, there were only the so called Rooms of Wonders, small spaces in which pieces collected throughout time by some naturalists, travelers or curiosities lovers were exhibited. The British Museum of London opened its doors in 1759 and Louvre Museum of Paris in 1793.

Curiosities. A famous Room of Wonders was the one belonging to Danish doctor Ole Worm. Created in 1654, it exhibited fossils and stuffed animals.

Academic Publications

Printed media consolidated itself as a key instrument for the dissemination of scientific knowledge. In the second half of the 19th century, science academies found it easier to publish magazines and articles, even though since the 17th century the journals of the most ancient institutions were in circulation, such as the Journal des Sçavans of the French Royal Academy of Sciences.

PRESENTATION
The just recently created (1666) Royal Academy of Sciences is presented to the king of France Louis XIV by its creator, Minister Jean-Baptiste Colbert.

Exhibitions

The easiest way to disseminate scientific advancements was directly showing the progress, thus, exhibitions in the most important cities of advanced countries became more habitual. Since 1851 the Universal Exhibitions began appearing, with a clear interest of spreading the development of science.

Electricity. The tower of Light of General Electric exhibited in the Chicago Exhibition (U.S.A.) of 1893.

Magazines for the Great Audience

The first scientific magazine aimed to the non specialized reader was Popular Science, founded in 1872 in the U.S.A. National Geographic Society magazine also appeared there in 1888, that even if it began as an academic magazine, it soon evolved towards the great audience, increasing from 1,400 copies in 1899 to 713,000 in 1920.

Renowned. Covers of *National Geographic Magazine* (1888, on the left, and 1889) and *Popular Science* (1931). They are both still published today.

Science in the Contemporary Age

Chapter 3

During the first two decades of the twentieth century, Albert Einstein's groundbreaking theories of relativity revolutionized the world of science, laying the foundations for nuclear energy and making the classical mechanics of Newton obsolete. In 1900, the German physicist Max Planck had already led the way with quantum mechanics (the branch of physics that studies the elementary particles and the structure of the atom), enriched with the subsequent contributions of Niels Bohr, Werner Heisenberg, Paul Dirac, Richard Feynman and others, besides Einstein himself. In 1929, Edwin Hubble and Milton Humason obtained the first observable evidence of the expansion of the universe. The Big Bang theory was established thereafter as the most accepted cosmological theory.

The advances in medical science have been overwhelming: from the revolution of antibiotics and genetic engineering to radiology and nuclear medicine, including transplants, implants and artificial insemination. Biomedicine became a speciality inside the clinical practice. The mapping of the human genome, publicly released in 2003, announces a future, no so far away, in which remedies for incurable or inherited diseases may be discovered in accordance with the genetic code of each person.

Freud and Psychology

The study of human behavior began its scientific stage, with the help of Sigmund Freud, in the late 19th century. The contributions of this Austrian physician, psychologist and thinker revolutionized our conception of the psyche.

The Father of Psychoanalysis

Grown in a Jewish family settled in Vienna, Sigmund Freud (1856-1939) developed the therapeutic technique known as psychoanalysis, designed to investigate the key factors in the thinking process and behavior of human beings. Freud also defined the structure of the human mind, which he divided into Id, Ego and Superego. During Nazism, his books were burned. In 1938, he left Vienna and moved to London, where he died.

Id, Ego and Superego

Freud divided the structure of the mind in three instances. In the depths of the psyche, according to him, one may find the Id, the impulses of instinct. It is unconscious and dominated by the pleasure principle. The Ego, conscious, comes behind it, controlling the desires and impulses of the Id. Finally, the Superego, mostly conscious, represents the authority and the rules received.

EGO

ID

SUPEREGO

The Legacy of Freud

Despite his controversial approaches, Freud marked psychiatry and psychology by providing a new conception for understanding personality. He developed the idea that personality is determined by repressed instincts, and he scientifically formulated the existence of the unconscious and the modus operandi of the mind.

VIENNA'S COUCH
Original sofa that patients used during psychotherapy sessions with Sigmund Freud.

AGAINST ALL ODDS
Freud had to battle with a hostile environment, in a repressed society that was scandalized by his ideas about sexual repression and religion.

Modern Psychology

Sigmund Freud and Wilhelm M. Wundt, German psychologist who founded the first laboratory of experimental psychology in 1877, were the parents of scientific psychology. The Viennese psychologist pioneered the use of clinical experience as a method for psychological research. This opened the door to other subsequent schools of psychology, such as the cognitive or humanistic one.

EPISTOLARY INFLUENCE
Through extensive correspondence, Freud influenced the prominent Swiss psychiatrist Karl Jung and had many disciples, including Alfred Adler or Sándor Ferenczi.

FUNDAMENTAL WORK
In 1899, he published his most important book, *The Interpretation of Dreams*, an analysis in which he applied his theory of unconscious impulses and desires. Other works such as *Three Essays on the Theory of Sexuality* (1905) and *Introduction to Psychoanalysis* (1916).

The Genius of Relativity

At the beginning of last century, the physicist Albert Einstein (1879–1955) altered with his theories of special and general relativity the notions of space, time and gravity that were considered definitely established since the time of Newton.

The Origin of Cosmology

In 1905, Albert Einstein postulated in his theory of special relativity that space and time are not absolute and independent of each other, but that they "melt" into a dynamic four-dimensional continuum called "space-time" which can be deformed as if it were a rubber band. A decade later, in 1915, Einstein included gravity to his theory (general relativity) and concluded that gravity is a consequence of the curvature of space-time. The ideas of the famous physicist served, among other things, to allow conceiving as the source of the expanding universe a big explosion or "Big Bang" and to believe in the existence of black holes formed by the collapse of stars.

$E = mc^2$

This famous equation made by Einstein, which relates mass and energy, was confirmed with the development of nuclear energy and atomic bombs. Paradoxically, Einstein was a pacifist committed to his time.

CURVED LINE
The path of the starlight is bent or "deflected" by the gravitational action of the Sun.

The Eclipse of 1919

On May 29, 1919, two scientific missions seized a solar eclipse to test Einstein's theory: if it was correct, the starlight should be displaced at a certain angle when passing near the Sun. One expedition observed the phenomenon in northern Brazil, and the other one, in West Africa. The solar gravitational field deflected starlight as Einstein had predicted and the German physicist became a world celebrity.

LUNAR SHADOW
Coming between the Sun and Earth, the Moon's shadow prevents the disturbance of sunlight and allows the stars to be visible during the day.

The Light Cone

The mathematician Hermann Minkowski (1864–1909) illustrated the concept of space–time of Einstein with a cone of light. It represents the evolution in time (past, present and future) of a light beam in a graph showing two of the three dimensions of space, the dimension of time and the observer at the origin of coordinates.

Future

Past

LETTER TO ROOSEVELT

In 1939, Einstein warned the U.S. president, Franklin D. Roosevelt that Germany could build an atomic bomb.

Star

Star

APPARENT POSITION

This is the notion of the star that is visible from Earth. The postulates of classical physics, however, held that in this case the Sun would prevent viewing both stars.

A SUPERIOR MIND

Albert Einstein had the ability to imagine experimental situations and draw original and daring conclusions, which he then translated into mathematical language. His contribution to theoretical physics and the study of the photoelectric effect won him the Nobel Prize in Physics of 1921.

General Theory of Relativity

Against the background of universal gravitation, Einstein thought of space linked to a dimension that was not contemplated by Newton: time. And gravity, which Newton believed to be a force that generated the attraction between two objects, was seen by Einstein as a consequence deriving from what he called the curvature of spacetime. In the theory of relativity, the universe is curved by the presence of objects of different masses. Gravity then is a spatial distortion.

Moon Landing

The space race between the U.S. and the Soviet Union led to the landing of the first man on the Moon in 1969. US citizen Neil Armstrong, one of the members of the Apollo 11 mission, was the first to leave a human footprint in outer space.

The Apollo Program

The U.S. Apollo 11 mission to the Moon lasted nearly 200 hours. For the trip, two modules were used, the orbital one (Columbia) and the lunar one (Eagle). Both were attached to the Saturn V rocket until it reached the desired speed. After making a correction of 180 degrees to reach the lunar orbit, the Eagle module was separated, with two astronauts aboard. It fired its engine and achieved Moon landing on July 20. The stay on the Moon lasted 21 hours and 38 minutes.

EAGLE LUNAR MODULE
It was divided into two parts, one for ascent and another for descent. It coupled with the orbital module, Columbia, in both the ascent and descent.

CABIN

2 In orbit
In 2 minutes and 42 seconds, the rocket reached a speed of 9,800 km/h and entered the Earth orbit.

Launch pad

1 Takeoff
The modules were powered by the Saturn V rocket, the heaviest ever built: nearly 3 million kilograms.

SATURN V
The rocket that propelled the Apollo and put it in orbit had a height equivalent to a 29-story building.

110 m

Turn

3 Impulse
The rocket turned around the Earth to gain impulse. The second stage is clear and the rocket reached 23,000 km/h.

OXYGENATOR TANK

EXPERIMENTAL EQUIPMENT

5 Separation
Once it reached lunar orbit, the Eagle module is detached and prepares its landing.

4 Linked modules
The orbital and lunar module are held together up to the trajectory correction.

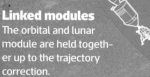

Correction

Eagle module

LM–5 EAGLE

- ▶ **Moon landing:** 20 July 1969
- ▶ **Module height:** 6.5 m
- ▶ **Weight:** 24,500 kg (4,100 kg on the Moon)
- ▶ **Cabin volume:** 6.65 m³
- ▶ **Crew:** 2 people

Historic Moment

The Apollo 11 mission left a series of historical prints, such as the image of the U.S. flag stack at the Moon symbolizing victory in the space race, or the footprint of Aldrin's boot (which was not the first, but one of them), representing the realization of a dream of man.

SPACE SHUTTLE

The creation, as from 1976, of the space shuttles was another great milestone. They were ships that could fulfil multiple missions in space.

OXYGEN GAS TANKS FOR IMPULSE

COLUMBIA ORBITAL MODULE

It remained in the orbit of the Moon to transport the Eagle back to Earth. It consisted of a command module and a service module.

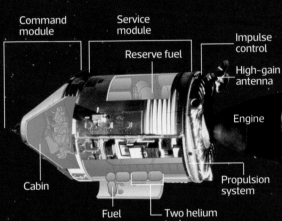

Command module

Service module

Reserve fuel

Impulse control

High-gain antenna

Engine

Cabin

Propulsion system

Fuel

Two helium tanks

VERY HIGH FREQUENCY ANTENNA

6.5 m

EAGLE

11 m

COLUMBIA

CSM-107 COLUMBIA

▸ **Launching:** 16 July 1969
▸ **Module height:** 11 m
▸ **Weight:** 30.000 kg
▸ **Cabin volume:** 6.2 m³
▸ **Crew:** 3 people

FUEL TANK

The Crew

The three members of the mission were already very experienced men at NASA. They all had participated in the Gemini program, key preparation to manage the landing and moonwalks.

Neil Armstrong (1930-2012)
In 1966, he performed his first mission aboard the Gemini VIII. He was the first man on the Moon.

Michael Collins (1930)
He was the third astronaut to perform a spacewalk, by means of the Gemini X mission. He was the pilot of the Columbia orbital module.

Edwin Aldrin (1930)
He participated in the training tasks of the XIII Gemini mission , and was the second man to set foot on lunar soil.

LANDING GEAR

Computer Science

By the middle of last century, a number of disciplines emerged devoted to the theoretical study of information processing and its application in computers. Today, the world is completely dependent on computer systems devised by these sciences.

Responding to Needs

Closely linked to other disciplines, such as mathematics or engineering, computer sciences aim to find solutions for any area of life, devising machines and programs that work with data processing. Driven by the development of electronics during the first third of the 20th century, the first computers were born in the forties, but were limited to the performance of automatic calculations. From there, its evolution was constant up to the current high levels of sophistication.

FATHER OF COMPUTING
Pioneer of computer science, English mathematician Alan Turing (1912-1954) conducted research on artificial intelligence and created a universal machine that served as the basis for subsequent computers.

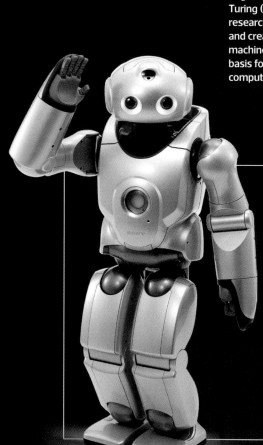

Artificial Intelligence

It is a concept that emerged in the fifties of last century as a branch of computer science. At first, the researchers approached the challenge with great optimism, but, over the years, the challenge of creating a machine that could "feel" and behave like a human being, revealed its complexity. Currently, there are robots with amazing qualities, but they merely generate the illusion of "living machines."

Humanoids. These are robots trying to resemble a human being. For now, commercial humanoids are used only for purposes of family entertainment.

MACHINE BEAT MAN
On February 10, 1996, an IBM computer called Deep Blue defeated world chess champion, Gary Kasparov, becoming the first computer to beat a reigning champion.

GIGANTIC
The first computers filled entire rooms, weighed tons and needed miles of cables to program them.

ENIAC

The ENIAC (Electronic Numerical Integrator And Computer), introduced in 1946, was one of the first electronic computers in history. It was built by the University of Pennsylvania for the U.S. Army and it occupied 167 m². This large machine of nearly 27 tons was able to calculate 5,000 additions and 300 multiplications per second.

Programming Languages

An object of constant study of computing has been the method to give orders to, or program, computers. Therefore, specific languages have been created, such as Fortran (first modern programming language), Cobol , Pascal, C, Basic, Java, HTML, Visual Basic, etc.

Punch cards. It was one of the first systems used to give instructions to computers.

Contemporary Medicine

Throughout the 20th century, drug development, understanding the immune system, the advent of genetics and the technological revolution of recent decades have given a great impulse to medicine, increasingly lengthening life expectancy.

Led by Technology

After the discovery of X-rays in 1895 (which allowed the observation within humans and the diagnosis of fractures and diseases), medicine experienced a new and decisive technological advance in the second half of the 20th century with the advent of improved tools and diagnostic techniques (such as computed axial tomography, magnetic resonance, ultrasound or flexible endoscopy), the manufacture of artificial organs and prostheses, and, in general , the application of computers to every area of this science. Definitely, surgery, which is increasingly less invasive and more effective, has been the field that has experienced more progress.

Computed Axial Tomography

The development of this technique in the 70s, which awarded the Nobel Prize for Medicine to A. M. Cormack and G. Hounsfield, was a turning point in the field of medical diagnosis. Thanks to a powerful X-ray scanner, tomography produces images of the inner body with incredible detail.

X-RAY BEAM

Ultrasound Scan

Convex probe. It is used in general and obstetric abdominal observation.

Developed in the 1950s based on the sonar, this test represents a breakthrough in the area of clinical diagnosis since it does not use radiation, but echoes. It is therefore ideal for viewing the evolution of **fetuses**, for which X-rays are harmful, and it also allows doing it in "real time."

New Diseases: AIDS

Throughout the 20th century, medicine has provided answers to many diseases by means of vaccines, but it has also had to cope with new ones, such as AIDS, identified in 1981. The advance of science has allowed this disease, caused by the HIV virus to the immune system, to go from being fatal to chronic, if combated with antiretroviral drugs.

REFRACTIVE SURGERY
After decades of refinement, laser eye surgery allows correcting defects of nearsightedness, farsightedness and astigmatism with simple operations and fast post-surgery recoveries.

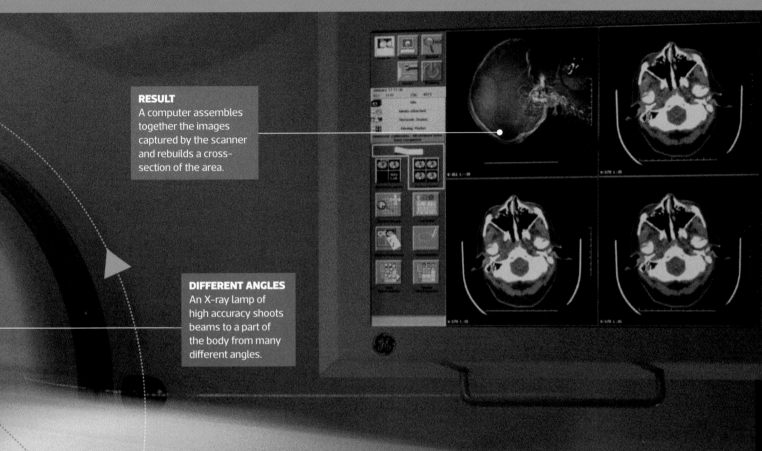

RESULT
A computer assembles together the images captured by the scanner and rebuilds a cross-section of the area.

DIFFERENT ANGLES
An X-ray lamp of high accuracy shoots beams to a part of the body from many different angles.

SENSOR
On the other hand, a sensor records the variations in light power. Each ray shows the average density of the area traversed.

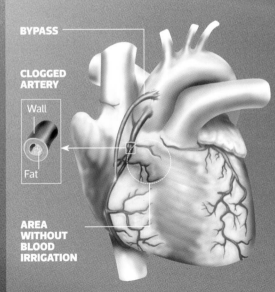

BYPASS

CLOGGED ARTERY

Wall

Fat

AREA WITHOUT BLOOD IRRIGATION

Cardiovascular Medicine

Heart-related diseases are the leading cause of death in developed countries; therefore, they have been subject to investigation and constant advances in recent decades. In 1958, internal pacemakers began being implanted and, in 1967, the first human heart transplant was performed.

Bypass. This technique, which revolutionized cardiovascular surgery, consists in creating an alternative blood route for a blocked artery.

Genetics

Although significant progress was already made in this branch of biology, such as the discovery of DNA molecules in the cells, it was in the second half of the 20th century when genetics experienced an overwhelming development, culminating in the deciphering of the human genome.

A Revolutionary Discovery

Since Gregor Mendel determined in the 19th century that organisms transmit a legacy of features, which was later known as genes, the scientific community did not rest until it achieved the deciphering of the secret best kept inside the cells: the genetic human map. In 1990, the Human Genome Project, a program with scientists from different countries, was aimed to reveal the complete DNA sequence of a human being, describing the more than 20,000 genes that comprise it. The objective was completed a decade later, and it represents one of the great milestones in the history of science.

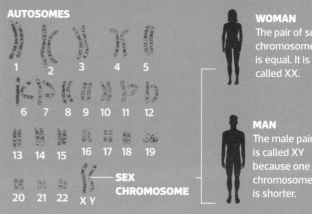

Human Chromosomes

Our genetic information is concentrated in 46 chromosomes: 22 pairs of autosomes and one pair of sex chromosomes, which differentiate men and women.

AUTOSOMES
1 2 3 4 5
6 7 8 9 10 11 12
13 14 15 16 17 18 19
20 21 22 X Y — **SEX CHROMOSOME**

WOMAN
The pair of sex chromosomes is equal. It is called XX.

MAN
The male pair is called XY because one chromosome (Y) is shorter.

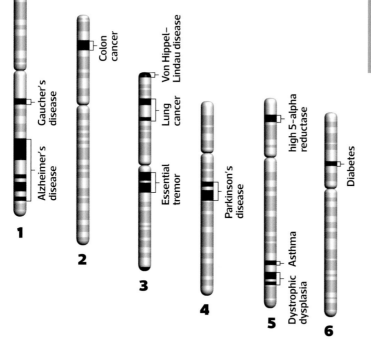

Chromosome labels:
- **1** — Alzheimer's disease, Gaucher's disease
- **2** — Colon cancer
- **3** — Von Hippel–Lindau disease, Lung cancer, Essential tremor
- **4** — Parkinson's disease
- **5** — high 5-alpha reductase, Asthma, Dystrophic dysplasia
- **6** — Diabetes
- **7** — Diabetes, Language development, Obesity
- **8** — Werner syndrome, Burkitt lymphoma
- **9** — Malignant melanoma, Blood group
- **10** — Mal de Refsum, Atrofia Girata
- **11** — Multiple endocrine neoplasia, Diabetes
- **12** — Zellweger syndrome

Chronology of genetics

1865	1889	1909	1926	1953	1973
Gregor Mendel This naturalistic monk discovered the laws of hereditary transmission through factors (genes).	**Chromosome** Wilhelm von Waldeyer names the structures forming the cellular DNA as chromosomes.	**Gene** William L. Johannsen gives the name gene to the smallest unit capable of encoding the entire protein.	**Genetic chain** Thomas Hunt Morgan shows that genes are joined in linkage groups inside the chromosomes.	**Double helix** James Watson and Francis Crick proposed a double-helix polymer model for the structure of DNA.	**Experiments** Successful tests of inserting genes from one species into the gene pool of another were conducted.

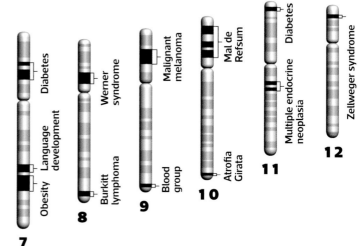

The Legacy of Mendel

One of the first naturalists to study genetic inheritance was Gregor Mendel, an Augustinian monk born in 1822 in Heinzendorf (then part of the Austrian Empire). Mendel postulated the laws of inheritance, which explain how physiological traits are transmitted from parents to children, from observations and experiments with peas, without even suspecting of the existence of DNA. He is considered the father of genetics.

The Gene Map

Sequencing established the location and function of genes in each chromosome, which allowed knowing, among other things, the origin of many diseases. It is known, for example, that about 1,400 genes cause inherited diseases. Scientists believe that a simple error in the sequence of a gene creates a predisposition to suffer a disease, crucial information to anticipate the diagnosis of diseases such as Alzheimer's, breast cancer, diabetes, etc. In addition, knowledge of the genome has opened new paths of research in the field of human evolution.

Muscular dystrophy

Sex determining factor

Fragile X syndrome

Y

X

DiGeorge syndrome

22

Amyotrophic lateral sclerosis

21

Severe combined immunodeficiency

20

Myotonic dystrophy

19

TRAIT THEORY
In 2006, a study concluded that the difference between the genome of two people can exceed 10%.

Memory

Mediterranean fever

Tumor-inhibiting protein

Breast cancer

Niemann-Picks Disease

18

17

Marfan syndrome

16

15

Breast cancer

Alzheimer's disease

14

Wilson's disease

13

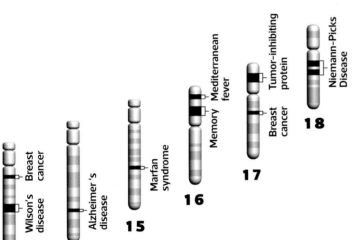

Alleles. Each parent contributes one to the children that can be dominant or recessive. The dominant one always prevails.

How Genes Are Transmitted

Each of the inherited traits is determined by the interaction of a pair of forms called alleles, located within the gene. Each parent contributes one to his/her children in such a manner that the so-called dominant one prevails over the recessive one.

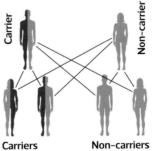

Carrier

Non-carrier

Carriers

Non-carriers

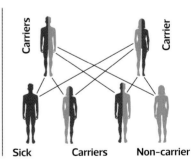

Carriers

Carrier

Sick

Carriers

Non-carrier

Diseases. If you have a genetic defect, a person can transmit a disease to his or her offspring.

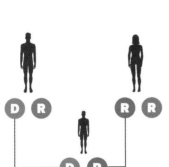

1975	1982	1990	1994	1997	2001
Sanger method F. Sanger developed a technique to decipher the sequence of the base DNA for the future Genome Project.	**Transgenic mouse** Dr. Palmiter showed in Nature magazine the first transgenic animal: a mouse with rat hormones.	**Genome Project** An international public consortium initiated a project to decipher the human genome in 15 years.	**Transgenic tomatoes** The commercialization of the first genetically engineered food is approved.	**Cloning** The birth of Dolly the sheep, the first cloned mammal, was announced a year earlier.	**Complete genome** The magazines *Science* and *Nature* simultaneously publish the complete sequence of the human genome.

Advances in Biomedicine

Genetic progress in recent decades and the continuing advances in technology have given a decisive impulse to molecular and cell biology, immunology and other branches that investigate the treatment of diseases.

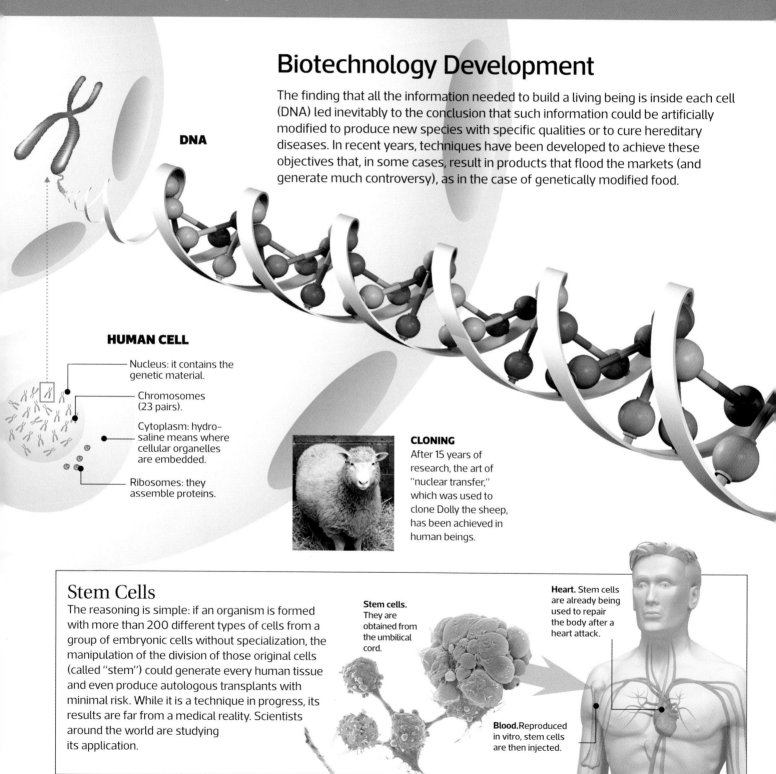

Biotechnology Development

The finding that all the information needed to build a living being is inside each cell (DNA) led inevitably to the conclusion that such information could be artificially modified to produce new species with specific qualities or to cure hereditary diseases. In recent years, techniques have been developed to achieve these objectives that, in some cases, result in products that flood the markets (and generate much controversy), as in the case of genetically modified food.

DNA

HUMAN CELL

Nucleus: it contains the genetic material.

Chromosomes (23 pairs).

Cytoplasm: hydro-saline means where cellular organelles are embedded.

Ribosomes: they assemble proteins.

CLONING
After 15 years of research, the art of "nuclear transfer," which was used to clone Dolly the sheep, has been achieved in human beings.

Stem Cells

The reasoning is simple: if an organism is formed with more than 200 different types of cells from a group of embryonic cells without specialization, the manipulation of the division of those original cells (called "stem") could generate every human tissue and even produce autologous transplants with minimal risk. While it is a technique in progress, its results are far from a medical reality. Scientists around the world are studying its application.

Stem cells. They are obtained from the umbilical cord.

Heart. Stem cells are already being used to repair the body after a heart attack.

Blood. Reproduced in vitro, stem cells are then injected.

Genetic Therapies

The first steps are being given in this new speciality that focuses on treating inherited diseases by modifications in the DNA of living people. Other medical conditions, such as cancer or AIDS, may also be treated with such therapies, which are under investigation in humans.

MODIFIED DNA

ADENOVIRUS

Introduction
The retrovirus introduces its now modified genetic material to the human cell.

3

4 **Result**
The cell works according to the new instructions.

2 **Modified**
The adenovirus DNA is modified to reduce its ability to cause diseases. At the same time, the DNA fragment to be inserted into the human cell is added.

CELL

1 **Vehicle**
An adenovirus is a non-enveloped icosahedral virus of double-stranded DNA, which causes many diseases. Modified to avoid being pathogen, they count with a region within that can transport a modified DNA sequence.

DNA STRUCTURE
This is a double helix in which the bases form "bridges," with an established order:

Cytosine ⎯⎯ Guanine

Adenine ⎯⎯ Thymine

Genetic Biochip

It is a tiny device containing biological material which is used for obtaining genetic information in order to diagnose diseases. When the biochip comes into contact with a sample of the patient, it interacts causing a characteristic pattern of light which is read by a scanner and interpreted by a computer.

SeroChip

BioChip

Current Astronomy

Thanks to the construction of increasingly powerful and sophisticated telescopes, some of them assembled on space satellites, in recent decades astronomy has made amazing advances in the understanding of the nature of the universe.

A Universe Discovered

Since 1925 when Edwin Hubble showed that the Universe was much larger than previously thought, astronomy has multiplied its progress. Today, the approximate age and composition of the universe is known, it is recognized that there are countless galaxies in it and about 700 planetary systems with nearly 900 planets (2013) were observed, dozens of them are very similar to Earth. But much remains to be discovered. Therefore, different telescopes and space probes track space.

Giant Telescopes

In the last fifty years, numerous astronomical observatories equipped with powerful telescopes have been built. Most of them are located in high areas of special atmospheric stability. This is the case of the Paranal Observatory (Chile), one of the most advanced observatories in the world thanks to the VLT, a set of four large reflecting telescopes of 8.2 m diameter.

Other observatories

Many plants respond to projects in participation with different countries that share the high costs of the telescopic technology, which is constantly updated.

Mauna Kea

It is a complex of observatories located on a volcano in Hawaii. It has the powerful optical telescopes Keck I and II.

Kitt Peak

It is located in the Sonoran Desert and has the largest solar telescope in the world, the McMath-Pierce.

Hubble Space Telescope

In 1990, NASA and the ESA put into orbit the Hubble Space Telescope, which represented one of the great milestones in the history of astronomy. For the first time, space images could be captured without the limitations of the atmosphere. The Hubble has been followed by other space telescopes like Kepler, exclusively dedicated to finding new exoplanets.

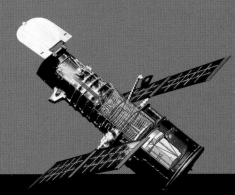

The Hubble. This Space Telescope orbits the Earth at around 600 km away. It has a mirror of 2.4 m in diameter

DOME
It protects and perceives any climate change through thermal sensors.

DSM
Beryllium deformable secondary mirror. It measures 1.1 m in diameter and has a thickness of only 2 mm.

Adjustment of the Optical Lens

The main feature of the VLT at Paranal is its revolutionary optical design. Thanks to the active and adaptive optics, it achieves resolution similar to the one it would achieve in space. To prevent the deformation of the primary mirror due to the force of gravity, the VLT has an active optics system that maintains the optimal mirror shape at all times thanks to 150 pistons that hold it and correct their position in a syncronized manner.

ACTIVE OPTICS

ADAPTIVE OPTICS

Incoming light

150-pistons cell

Light beam reflected

Curved mirror

Incorrect vision

Correct vision

VLT (Very Large Telescope). Telescope of the ESO (European Southern Observatory) in the Chilean Paranal Observatory.

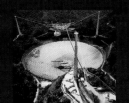

Arecibo
The giant radio telescope observatory on the island of Puerto Rico has a diameter of 305 m.

ALMA
Opened in 2013 in the Atacama Desert (Chile), this observatory has the world's largest telescope.

Roque de los Muchachos
Located in the Canary Islands (Spain), it houses telescopes -mostly night telescopes- of up to 19 different nationalities.

Eco Challenge

In the middle of last century, the scientific community awoke environmental awareness of the world alerting of the serious deterioration the planet was suffering by human action. Since then, ecology as a science took on a new dimension.

The Harmful Action of Man

After years of analysis and research, studies such as *Silent Spring* (1962) by the biologist Rachel Carson managed to raise international ecological awareness by denouncing the enormous prejudice caused by the emission of gases and industrial waste, the intensive exploitation of resources, the use of pesticides and sprays, deforestation, etc., which caused severe alterations in the biosphere, such as global warming, the hole in the ozone layer or desertification. As a result, environmental movements proliferated gaining more representation in politics.

GAIA HYPOTHESIS
English chemist James Lovelock (1919), one of the fathers of modern ecology, launched in 1969 his controversial Gaia Hypothesis, according to which the Earth is a self-regulating living being, that maintains adequate conditions for all the organisms that inhabit it.

Earth Goddess. Lovelock next to a statue of the goddess Gaia, after whom his hypothesis was named.

Sustainable solutions
Ecology claims that if current human development parameters are maintained, the survival of man on Earth is in danger. Against this, it proposes:

1 Reduction of CO_2 emissions
It is vital to use cleaner sources of energy (wind, solar, hydro, etc.) of biofuel or "green" transport powered by electricity, for example.

2 Controlling pollution
The air, soil and water increasingly receive chemicals from industrial emissions and discharges and intensive agriculture (fertilizers, herbicides).

3 Recycling
Mankind produces thousands of tons of garbage daily, and a great part of it is toxic or of slow decomposition. Recycling is the only short term solution.

4 Protection of biodiversity
Many species and ecosystems are disappearing. It is essential to identify and protect areas at risk and to avoid overusing resources (timber, fishing, etc.).

The Hole in the Ozone Layer
Man-made substances are destroying the ozone layer that protects us from ultraviolet rays, which increasingly exposes us to certain diseases such as skin cancer. The evolution of this phenomenon is evident in the poles.

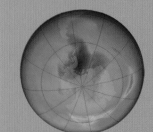
September 17, 1979

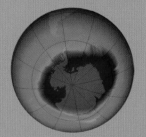
October 1, 2010

The Green Revolution
Between the 1960s and 1990s, in developing countries, especially in Asia and Latin America, there was a large increase in agricultural production. It was known as the Green Revolution and it was based on innovations such as the use of high yielding varieties (HYV), monoculture, widespread irrigation and mechanization. All this was determined by the massive use of pesticides and fertilizers and with the consequent ecological damage.

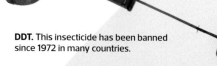

DDT. This insecticide has been banned since 1972 in many countries.

The Green Front

In recent decades, the number of organizations dedicated to defending and protecting the environment has steadily increased. Some more militant than others, as Greenpeace, have been influential by shocking campaigns to reverse harmful situations, such as indiscriminate whaling.

WHAT IS ECOLOGY?
The term, coined by German Ernst Haeckel in 1869, refers to the science that studies the relationship between living things and their environment.

Desertification

It is one of the workhorses of ecology. Indiscriminate logging, population growth and intensive farming turn formerly fertile regions into deserts.

Madagascar. It is the most eroded country in the world. 93 % of its temperate forests have been logged.

The Greenhouse Effect

It is the name given to the capacity of certain gases in the atmosphere to retain heat that the sun irradiates on Earth. This phenomenon, exacerbated by human activity, is responsible for the global warming that the planet is experiencing, and consequently, for the melting of the poles, the rising sea levels, the change in weather patterns and habits of some species, etc.

SUNRAYS
They transverse the atmosphere and reach the Earth's surface almost unhindered.

ON EARTH
Clouds, oceans and land absorb some of the solar radiation, becoming warmer. An important part is reflected in the form of heat.

ALBEDO
About 30 % of the solar radiation that reaches Earth is reflected by the planet and sent back to space.

HEATING
Most of the radiation reflected by the Earth is returned back to the earth's surface by greenhouse gases. This process heats the planet and the atmosphere even more.

LESS INTENSITY
The infra-red beams (heat) bounce once and again, warming the planet's surface, but with increasingly less efficiency.

ATMOSPHERE

GREENHOUSE GASES

LAND AREA

Geosciences

The Earth sciences or geosciences are a group of disciplines in charge of the study of the internal structure, morphology and evolution of the planet, as well as all processes occurring in the geosphere, hydrosphere and atmosphere.

Preventing the Future

Beyond the simple desire for knowledge, geosciences study nature and the dynamics of the planet in the past and the present in order to anticipate future behavior. The aim is twofold: first, to foresee natural disasters such as earthquakes, hurricanes and tsunamis, and secondly, to accurately plan the exploitation of natural resources. For such purpose, it is key to collect the maximum possible amount of data in different media – land, water and air– and process it, a task that has gained efficiency over time thanks to continuous technological advances.

WEATHER CENTRALS
They standardize the data obtained in different cities around the world and promote the application of forecasts for various human activities.

Geophysics, Geology and Geography

These are the major disciplines devoted to the analysis of the structure, the evolution and behavior of the soil and terrestrial subsoil. They allow, for example, understanding and anticipating natural disasters such as earthquakes or volcanic eruptions.

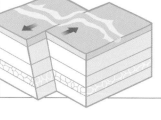

Seismology. Branch of geophysics which deals with the study of earthquakes, faults and other terrestrial phenomena.

WEATHER STATION
The ground-level observations provide partial data. Besides the thermometer, a hygrometer and barometer are used, which measure, respectively, humidity and atmospheric pressure.

Sounder. Most ships carry an echo sounder on their hulls, which measures depth.

Oceanography

This branch of geography and geoscience studies all the physical, biological, geological and chemical processes that occur in oceans and seas. It analyses, for example, tides, currents, pits and coastal formations.

Underwater vehicle. It takes pictures to measure the physical properties of seawater (temperature, salinity, density, etc.), which are then forwarded by GPS.

In the Atmosphere

Data can be collected by aircraft, satellites or radiosondes, which immediately transmit the information to the weather stations. Radiosondes reach up to 15,000 m in height, while a single satellite can cover the entire land area.

ARTIFICIAL SATELLITES
They provide images that are used for the visualization of clouds, water vapor existing in the atmosphere and for measuring the temperatures of land and ocean surfaces.

WEATHER AIRCRAFT
It provides data on temperature and humidity. It takes pictures of the particles contained in clouds.

RADIOSONDES
They can travel in hot air balloons or be dropped from an airplane. They collect data on temperature, pressure and humidity at different heights. They also indicate the direction and speed of wind.

P-3 HURRICANE HUNTER AIRCRAFT
Its doppler radars have a resolution that is four times greater than that of a standard doppler radar of conventional use. They can exceed 4,000 m in height.

AEROSONDE
It provides weather information at intervals of tenths of a second

Meteorology and Climatology

These are two main branches of Earth sciences since they are responsible for analysing and forecasting weather and its variations in the short-term (meteorology) and over time (climatology). The development of these two disciplines is vital to many human activities, such as agriculture, but mainly to prevent disasters related to weather phenomena.

Weather buoy. It is used to know the conditions of the sea in areas that are not covered by boats.

Maritime probe. It is launched from an airplane and it sinks into the sea to determine soil depth. It is no longer used.

RADAR STATION
It is used to know the intensity with which rain, snow or ice fall. The radar sends waves that bounce off on the raindrops and return to a receiver screen.

Global Projects

As science has become more complex, collaboration between researchers from different disciplines and countries has become more widespread. Today, in areas such as particle physics, it is not strange that a work is signed by over a hundred authors.

Science Without Borders

The Large Hadron Collider (LHC) of the European Organization for Nuclear Research (CERN) is perhaps the most monumental scientific project of all time. It is a circular particle accelerator, of 9 km in diameter, located underground on the border between France and Switzerland, and it is the perfect example of international collaboration between members of the scientific community. Its scientists study subatomic particles, while recreating the conditions of the Big Bang. Such an undertaking was made possible through the collaboration of physicists, astrophysicists, mathematicians and nuclear engineers from almost fifty countries.

SUPERCONDUCTING MAGNETS
It received contributions from all countries, but especially from Finland, France, Italy, Japan, Korea, Switzerland and the US.

HADROM CALORIMETRE
Contributions from Bulgaria, India, Spain, the US, Belarus, Russia and Ukraine.

The CMS Detector
This instrument, with a weight of 12,500 tons, is designed to analyse, during collisions between protons at very high energies, the generated particles (such as photons, muons and other fundamental particles) and aspects related to their mass, energy and speed. 36 countries, 160 institutions and 2,008 scientists participated in its construction.

21.5 m

15 m

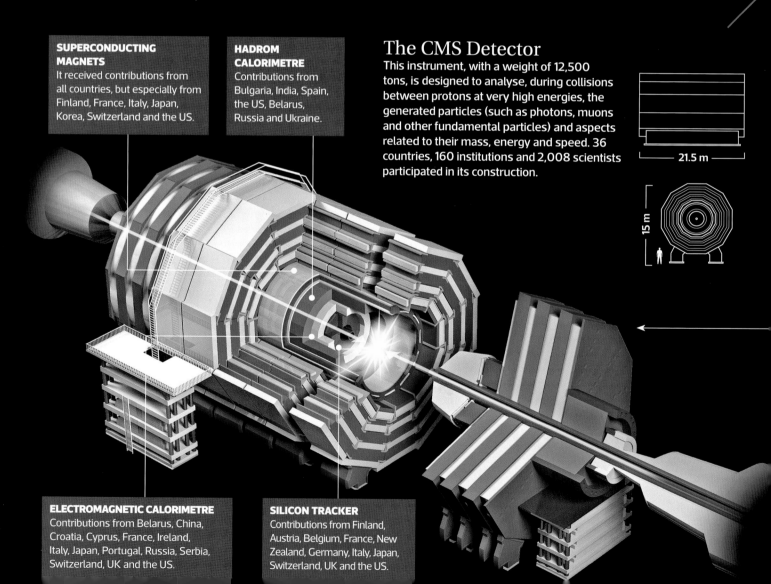

ELECTROMAGNETIC CALORIMETRE
Contributions from Belarus, China, Croatia, Cyprus, France, Ireland, Italy, Japan, Portugal, Russia, Serbia, Switzerland, UK and the US.

SILICON TRACKER
Contributions from Finland, Austria, Belgium, France, New Zealand, Germany, Italy, Japan, Switzerland, UK and the US.

The ATLAS Detector

It is one of the five detectors that are part of the Large Hadron Collider. This is a tool designed to explore the fundamental nature of matter and the basic forces that govern the universe as from particle collisions. It weighs 7,000 tons (a weight equivalent to 60 diesel locomotives).

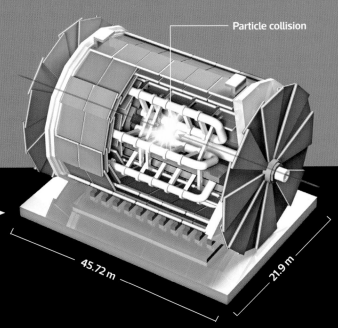

Particle collision

45.72 m

21.9 m

PS

1

2

ATLAS

2.25 km

ALICE

LHC-b

3

8.53 km

4

Heavy ions (more than one proton)..

27 km

CMS

Large Hadron Collider

In the LHC, protons at very high energies are "smashed" against other protons or against heavier ions (consisting of several protons). When particles "break" as a result of collisions, fundamental particles of the universe are generated during millionths of a second.

1 Linear particle accelerator
In it, the nuclei of the atoms are separated from the electrons, which turns them into ions.

2 Great acceleration
The ions are energized and accelerated up to speeds approaching that of light.

3 Radio Waves
Powerful strokes of radio waves raise the energy of ions to two billion electron volts (an energy value of large magnitude).

3 Million of ions
The ions, which are now very highly energized, are introduced in clusters of billions of units in the accelerator, going in opposite directions.

Remarkable Collaborative Efforts

The struggle against diseases, climate change or space exploration are some of the fields that gather international scientific cooperation.

1990	2000	2000	2008
IPCC Hundreds of scientists from the Intergovernmental Panel or Group on Climate Change (IPCC) confirmed their concern about climate change of human origin. The IPCC received the Nobel Peace Prize in 2007.	**Genome Project** Thousands of scientists from 18 different countries and belonging to two separate private and public finance groups completed the draft for the genome sequence of a human being.	**Space station** The first crew arrived to the International Space Station, a joint venture of five space agencies. To date, it has been visited by astronauts from more than 15 countries.	**Pierre Auger** The Pierre Auger Observatory was opened in Malargüe (Mendoza, Argentina): a joint initiative involving some 400 scientists from 20 countries in order to detect cosmic rays.

Science and Ethics

The scientific activity requires an ethical regulation that prevents governments and individuals from using it in experiments or in any type of project that is detrimental to the health of some people or society in general.

Unspoken Rules

Scientific ethics can have two areas: internal and external. The internal ethics is necessary for the proper functioning of science and consists of unspoken rules of the scientific community that no researcher should violate. For example, the prohibition of fraud, plagiarizing the work of others and evidence tampering. External scientific ethics, however, deals with the impact of science on society or the environment. For example, the prohibition of experimenting with humans without their consent, reducing the suffering of laboratory animals and the promotion of environmental care.

Scientific Deceptions

Among the most famous cases of fraud are the one by palaeoanthropologist Charles Dawson, who in 1912 presented the jaw of an orangutan as evidence of the missing link, or the recent falsification by South Korean scientist Hwang Woo Suk of the result of his experiments with stem cells.

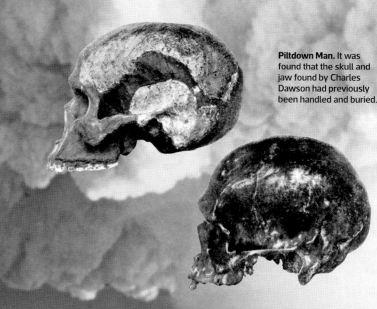

Piltdown Man. It was found that the skull and jaw found by Charles Dawson had previously been handled and buried.

"Prescribed babies." Also called "savior siblings," they are conceived through in vitro fertilization with the sole purpose of donating stem cells or other tissue for a sick relative.

Amid Controversy

Topics as diverse as human cloning, transplants, euthanasia, nuclear energy, climate change, stem cells and neuroscience generate controversy and debates in society. This has led every research center to usually have an ethics committee, able to guide and help said center in the making of appropriate decisions.

Genetic modifications. Transgenic bodies are organisms the genome of which was altered in the laboratory in order to provide specific new features. It has been done in living organisms and food.

States and Scientific Ethics

In Nazi Germany, physician Josef Mengele, the "angel of death," performed cruel experiments on inmates of Auschwitz (Poland). But Germany is not the only country that has skipped the "principles" of science. The U.S. CIA itself has conducted unimaginable practices.

CIA'S MKULTRA
During the Cold War, the Central Intelligence Agency of the U.S. developed scientific programs of questionable ethics, such as MKULTRA.

Atomic Bomb. On August 6, 1945, it was confirmed in Hiroshima (Japan) how destructive science can be if misused.

Science and Weapons

By its devastating consequences, the creation of the atomic bomb is the highlight of science misuse for armament purposes by governments. In 1943, a group of the best physicists in the world was gathered in a laboratory at Los Alamos to secretly build the first atomic bomb. Around 150,000 people participated in the so-called Manhattan Project, which ended with the launching of the first two atomic bombs of uranium and plutonium on the Japanese cities of Hiroshima and Nagasaki in 1945.

THE FATHER OF NUCLEAR FISSION
The demonstration, in 1939, that the uranium-235 atom could be fissioned and the discovery, in 1940, of plutonium-239 facilitated the work of Enrico Fermi, an Italian physicist exiled in the U.S. Fermi built the first nuclear reactor in history at the University of Chicago.

Nuclear Disasters

While they provide much of the electricity needed to make everything work and even if they are an alternative to fossil fuels, nuclear energy and thermal power mega-dams still are controversial: they generate radioactive waste that can last 20,000 years and are capable of causing major human and ecological disasters.

CHERNOBYL (1986)
The plant in the Ukrainian town of Chernobyl was the protagonist, on April 26, 1986, of the worst nuclear accident in the 20th century, with an impact on the environment that still persists. The cause was a poorly conducted experiment, in which numerous safety standards were violated. The resulting toxic cloud reached half of Europe.

FUKUSHIMA (2011)
In March 2011, the Japanese city of Fukushima experienced the worst nuclear accident since the Chernobyl disaster. After an earthquake and a tsunami, the cooling systems of the plants failed and there were water leaks with radioactive material. 200,000 people were evacuated. The Fukushima I plant only had a retaining wall that was 6 m tall despite being in an area facing the risk of large tsunamis.

Scientific Activism

Individually or collectively, renown scientists and anonymous people perform actions with the aim of a better world. This is the case of Jane Goodall who, besides her remarkable scientific contributions, helped to the conservation of the natural environment and wildlife.

Jane Goodall and Chimpanzees

Born in 1934, this British primatologist and naturalist devoted much of her life to the study of chimpanzees. For half a century, she observed the behavior of this species in Gombe Stream (Tanzania), and she found that, contrary to what was thought, chimpanzees were able to use and make tools. After leaving Africa, Goodall was dedicated to spread throughout the world the message of wildlife and environment conservation and to promote sustainable lifestyles.

TO A DISTANCE
Goodall began her observations from afar with binoculars. In two years, the animals were habituated to her presence and she earned their trust.

"HUMAN" BEHAVIORS
The primatologist observed chimpanzees' behaviors expressing cruelty, aggression, solidarity, affection and she even confirmed the adoption of younger chimpanzees.

Contributions
Thanks to Goodall's field work in Gombe we know that chimpanzees are not herbivores: she saw a group of males eating a female of another community, as well as smaller mammals and insects. She also witnessed attacks between different groups.

For a Better World

As in the case of Jane Goodall, many other projects and individual or small anonymous group struggles have become over time causes at a global scale, which have helped to improve society or to benefit the environment. In the field of scientific activism, some names like Barry Commoner, founder of the global environmental movement, are highlighted.

Barry Commoner. His great worth as a scientist was no obstacle to his political commitment and fierce defence of the environment.

Disguised as "Dolly." Greenpeace activists protest in Munich against patents on life.

Activism and Society

The scientific activity today stands at a confluence of economic, political and ethical concerns, among others. Social movements are involved in science, and vice versa, the commitment to science can create said movements. Some activists have protested, for example, against the possibility of obtaining pharmaceutical patents on life: embryos, genes, human organs and limbs from humans or other living beings.

HABITAT
In 1977, Goodall created the Institute that bears her name and began a campaign to warn of the destruction of the habitat of chimpanzees and their use in experiments.

SKILLS
Goodall discovered that chimpanzees were able to use twigs to extract honey or hunt termites, and stones to crack nuts.

Glossary

ALCHEMY The practice of converting base metals into gold or to find a universal elixir.

CARTOGRAPHY The practice of drawing maps.

DEDUCE To arrive at a conclusion by reasoning.

ECLIPSE The phenomenon when light from one celestial body is obscured by the passage of another between it and the observer or between it and its source of illumination.

EMPIRICAL Based on observation or experience rather than theory or pure logic.

EQUINOX The time or date when the sun crosses the celestial equator, when day and night are of equal length.

GENOME The complete set of genes or genetic material in a cell or organism.

HELIOCENTRIC Relating to the sun as the center.

HIERARCHY The classification of things according to relative importance.

INFINITESIMAL An indefinitely small quantity.

METALLURGY The branch of science and technology concerned with the properties of metals.

MORPHOLOGY The study of the structure of animals and plants

NEOLITHIC Relating to the later part of the Stone Age.

OPHTHALMOLOGY The science of the treatment of disorders and diseases of the eye.

PALEOLITHIC Relating to the early phase of the Stone Age.

PAPYRUS A material prepared in ancient Egypt used throughout the ancient Mediterranean world for writing or painting on.

PARCHMENT A material made from the prepared skin of an animal and used as a writing surface.

PAROCHIAL Relating to a church parish.

PNEUMATIC Operated by gas under pressure.

SEXAGESIMAL A numeral system with sixty as its base.

SOOTHSAYER A person who is believed to foresee the future.

THEOREM Truth established by means of accepted truths.

TRIGONOMETRY The mathematics that deals with the relations of the sides and angles of triangles and with the relevant functions of any angles.

ZOOLOGY The study of the behavior of animals.

Association of Science – Technology Centers

818 Connecticut Avenue, NW

7th Floor

Washington, DC 20006-2734

(202) 783-7200

Website: www.astc.org

Through strategic alliances and global partnerships, the Association of Science-Technology Centers (ASTC) strives to increase awareness of the valuable contributions its members make to their communities and the field of informal STEM learning.

Canada Science and Technology Museum

P.O. Box 9724, Station T

Ottawa, Ontario K1G 5A3

Canada

866) 442-4416

Website: Website: cstmuseum.techno-science.ca

The Canada Science and Technology Museum is the largest of its kind in Canada, and fulfills its mission through its collection, its permanent, temporary and traveling exhibitions, as well as special events, school programs, and workshops.

Liberty Science Center

Liberty State Park 222

Jersey City Boulevard

Jersey City, NJ 07305

(201) 200-1000

Website: www.lsc.org

Liberty Science Center is a 300,000-square-foot learning center dedicated to bringing the excitement of science to people of all ages.
Museum of Science and Industry, Chicago

5700 S Lake Shore Drive

Chicago, IL 60637

(773) 684-1414

Website: www.msichicago.org

The Museum of Science and Industry, Chicago is home to more than 400,000 square feet of hands-on exhibits designed to spark scientific inquiry and creativity.

WEBSITES

Because of the changing nature of internet links, Rosen Publishing has developed an online list of websites related to the subject of this book. This site is updated regularly. Please use this link to access the list:

http://www.rosenlinks.com/VHW/science

DK Publishing. *Timelines of Science.* New York, NY: DK Publishing, 2013.

Bauer, S W. *The Story of Western Science: From The Writings of Aristotle to the Big Bang Theory.* New York, NY: W.W. Norton & Company, 2015.

Bynum, W. F. *A Little History of Science.* New Haven, CT: Yale University Press, 2012.

Dolnick, Edward. *The Clockwork Universe: Isaac Newton, The Royal Society, And The Birth Of The Modern World.* New York, NY: HarperCollins, 2011.

Goddard, Jolyon. *Concise History of Science & Invention: An Illustrated Time Line.* Washington, D.C: National Geographic, 2010.

Kuhn, Thomas S., And Ian Hacking. *The Structure of Scientific Revolutions. Chicago.* London, England: The University of Chicago Press, 2012.

Mukherjee, Siddhartha. *The Gene: An Intimate History.* New York, NY: Scribner, 2016.

Newton, Isaac, Et Al. *The Principia Mathematical Principles of Natural Philosophy.* Berkeley: University of California Press, 1999.

Weinberg, Steven. *To Explain the World: The Discovery of Modern Science.* New York: Harper, 2015.

Wootton, David. *The Invention of Science: A New History of the Scientific Revolution.* New York, NY: HarperCollins Publishers, 2015.

Index